To Speak of this Land

To Speak of this Land

Identity and Belonging in South Africa and Beyond

Duncan Brown

UKZN PRESS University of KwaZulu-Natal Press

Published in 2006 by University of KwaZulu-Natal Press
Private Bag X01, Scottsville, 3209
South Africa
Email: books@ukzn.ac.za
Website: www.ukznpress.co.za

ISBN 1-86914-081-8

Editor: Andrea Nattrass
Cover designer: Sebastien Quevauvilliers, Flying Ant Designs
Typesetter: Patricia Comrie
Back cover drawing: A porcupine's hole with tracks, drawn by /Han≠kass'o on 4 September 1878 (courtesy of the Bleek and Lloyd Archives, Jagger Library, University of Cape Town)

Printed and bound by Interpak Books, Pietermaritzburg

Contents

For Hugh and Jean Brown

And she's walking in a dream listening
For that special sound
The echo of the plough whip over
Weenen county ground.
'Weenen county you took my man' she says
'You took my home, you took my land
You left me all alone – now I'm coming home.'
Weenen County in the springtime
Hadedas on the wing.

Juluka, 'Mama Shabala' (*African Litany*, 1981)

Out there in Jutland
In the old man-killing parishes
I will feel lost,
Unhappy and at home.

Seamus Heaney, 'The Tollund Man' (*Wintering Out*, 1972: 48)

He had plenty of thoughtful gripes about change made and change unmade, but he made what to this day remains the single most powerful comment ever made on the *Trek*.

He had been talking about problems. He'd failed to mention that he was about to quit university despite a series of strong passes because his pensioner parents couldn't muster the money, and stuck instead to public difficulties. I said: 'Given all these problems that you identify, has the change been meaningful to you?'

He drew a big breath and said, 'I belong.' In print, like this, that looks like not much. But there you have the pallor of print versus the trenchancy the box can produce. The way Tuna said it, deep, rolling, erupting from the depths of his history, half smiling and half daring . . . ag Tuna, you're one of those people who make this nation so exciting.

Denis Beckett, *Trekking* (1996: 46)

. . . my chest hurts with the indescribable intimacy of belonging and loss.
Antjie Krog, *A Change of Tongue* (2003: 36)

Something like a sense of place kicked in when I moved here, and I realized that I felt genuinely comfortable for the first time in my life.
John Gierach, *Death, Taxes and Leaky Waders* (2002: 310)

It is my feeling . . . that if anyone, anywhere, anytime, feels fully 'at home', they are not paying attention.
Stephen Clingman, 'Bram Fischer and the Question of Identity' (2004: 61)

Acknowledgements

This book has been some years in the writing, and I am grateful to a number of people who have assisted me in various ways.

To David Attwell, Don Beale, Elana Bregin, Tracey Brown, Michael Chapman, Margaret Daymond, Ileana Dimitriu, Craig Duvel, Michael Falkson, Michael Green, Liz Gunner, Johan Jacobs, Alan James, Antjie Krog, Ashlee Lenta, Margaret Lenta, Sally-Ann Murray, Jeff Opland, David Richards, Cheryl Stobie and Gerald West for their comments on all or part of the manuscript; and to my colleagues, past and present, in English Studies at the University of KwaZulu-Natal for the stimulating discussions of many of the ideas with which I engage in this book.

To Jeff Opland for providing me with access to his translations of the Nontsizi Mgqwetho material; John Vinnicombe, André Truter, Windhoek Kamijola, Juoa Antonio and Kaskorino Viljoen for the time they spent assisting me with my research in Underberg; Hein Willemse for advising me about some of the translations; Lance Stehr and Delphine Klassen for their assistance at Ghetto Ruff records; the staff at the National English Literary Museum (NELM) for assisting me in locating much of the material on Mazisi Kunene; Bernth Lindfors for information about the manuscript of *Emperor Shaka the Great*; and Ronnie Govender, Mazisi Kunene and the late Douglas Livingstone for discussing their work with me.

To those students of the University of Natal and the University of KwaZulu-Natal with whom I have shared many of these ideas, and who have helped to shape and modify my thinking.

To Michael and Tracey for their love and support, ever offered, never taken for granted and always cherished.

To my parents Hugh and Jean, to whom this book is dedicated. They taught me so much about the knowledge and love of place, and would be delighted that it was completed about thirty kilometres from my mother's birthplace, and about the same distance from the railway station where they first met.

To Andrea Nattrass for her superb editing and advice.

To the National Research Foundation and the Research Office of the University of KwaZulu-Natal for financial support. Opinions expressed are my own and are not necessarily to be attributed to either of these organisations.

* * *

The author and publishers gratefully acknowledge permission from the following people and organisations to reproduce material in this book: Jeff Opland for excerpts from translations of the Nontsizi Mgqwetho material; Michael Chapman for extracts from his critical writing; Monica Fairall for sections of the Douglas Livingstone poems; Ronnie Govender for excerpts from his short stories; the Wesleyan Press for material from Tricia Rose; and Lance Stehr at Ghetto Ruff Records for quotations from the Prophets of da City lyrics.

Earlier versions of, or extracts from, chapters in this book have appeared as journal articles. Thanks to the editors and referees of the following journals: *English in Africa*; *African Literature Today*; *Critical Arts*; *Current Writing*; *Semeia*; and *Moving Worlds*.

From //Kabbo to Zapiro

A Foreword

One of our country's earliest stories was told by //Kabbo through Wilhelm Bleek and Lucy Lloyd. In a thoroughly postmodern way //Kabbo dictated to them that they should write down that he was wanting to return to the place of his family and his ancestors; the moment the moon turned, he would be going. He interspersed his wish with an analysis of his situation at his neglected homestead where whites had moved onto his land, turning his people into fearful and hungry beings. He spelt out his wishes for shoes and a gun, while at the same time analysing whites (whom he did not regard as 'fellowmen') as people who did not have their own stories, who only talked their own language, who only visited their own kind and who used others to prepare their food. All of this was dictated by //Kabbo and faithfully recorded and translated by Bleek and Lloyd.

It is the rarest and most moving of stories.

In a fascinating discussion Duncan Brown points out how this text reveals that //Kabbo found binary choices unhelpful. Instead of being trapped in a particular mode of doing, //Kabbo moved across divisions 'that are often held to be absolute: orality/literacy; tradition/modernity; prehistory/history'. //Kabbo did not see his 'appropriation of Western technological modernity in any way contradicting or undermining his /Xam understanding of the world.'

This forms a sharp contrast to the Western mindset that often regards entries from developing worlds as contaminating and compromising ‘standards’. Even today, in a world where people are obsessed with ‘their’ world, ‘their’ history, ‘their’ religion, ‘their’ language, //Kabbo’s words are a sharp reminder of how narrow these criteria are. I am left with a feeling that the /Xam were living according to a world-view that was in many ways much too sophisticated to survive the brutality of white settlers.

Then Brown takes an unexpected turn, as he does in many of the chapters in this book. He looks at the art of tracking, of ‘reading’ the spoor of animals while at the same time mapping out possible scenarios, and discusses these complicated processes. Readers become acutely aware of a highly intricate ability about which they likely know absolutely nothing.

* * *

There once was a Basotho chief, writes Eugene Casalis, a missionary under Moshoeshoe, who met with the white men who had simply settled on his land. These men were determined to force the chief to draw a border between them, so that they could claim possession of the territory they were in.

> ‘Listen,’ said this chief, ‘to a story which is, I am told, in your great Book: It happened once that two women disputed about a child before a very wise king. The latter ordered the child to be cut in two, and half to be given to each of the women. ‘It is quite just,’ said the pretended mother! ‘Let it be divided instantly!’ ‘Oh no!’ cried the real mother, ‘I would rather lose it entirely!’ . . . You my friends, who are strangers, you think it quite natural that my ground should be cut. I who am born here, I feel my soul revolt at the thought. No; I will not cut it! Better lose it altogether!’ (1965: 157)

What is happening in this short paragraph written by Casalis is quite astonishing. On one level it is an old South African story: land appropriation accompanied by the appropriators’ desire to have their theft officially endorsed by those whom they had taken from.

In 1838 Dingane simply rounded up Piet Retief and his men and killed them, leaving the 'sales' document to rot with the corpses. But the Basotho chief described by Casalis decided to tell a story in order to describe the situation.

He could have given the men a lecture in Basotho ownership and land tenure. He could have explained the history of the Basotho in terms of sharing. He could have told them how land, like the sky, could not and should not be owned. He could have told them the famous *litsomo* (folk narrative) of Kodumodumo, a monster that devoured the whole Basotho nation.

Instead, he decided not to tell them *his* story, but to tell them *their* story – to give them, as it were, their own story back – as if he realised that those in front of him were incapable of understanding anybody else's story. If you want someone to understand you clearly, you can only do it through *their* story.

Although the Basotho chief and the white settlers were concerned with land, by using a non-land story from the Bible the chief achieved four things: he had immediate access to his listeners; he turned his claim to the land into divine providence; he expressed his biological and emotional link to the land by using a mother and child image; and he turned a history of greed and appropriation into a history of integrity and sacrifice.

The paragraph concludes with the chief pointing out that the request was not merely a contestation about land, but was pitching those whose souls revolted at the thought of dividing their land against 'you my friends, who are strangers'.

Despite being master of the telling, the chief was experiencing a triple tragedy. His foreboding that he was soon to lose his land, as had other chiefs around him, must have been greatly aggravated by the fact that he had to use his enemy's story to convey his deep and legitimate claim to the land. But the biggest tragedy was that, unlike in the Bible story, there was no wise king to sit in judgement on the situation.

* * *

I remember running a student poetry workshop in a township of Welkom in the mid-1980s. One of the exercises was that students should sit facing the open *veld* (countryside) across the schoolyard and write a poem about what they saw. After a while one of them threw down his pencil. When I inquired about his actions, he said: 'Why should I write about *your* land?'

I remember that in 1995 the editor of the weekly *Mail & Guardian* newspaper asked a few writers to write about the new South Africa. The whites wrote about the past; the blacks described the landscape.

I remember a plant-trail brochure at the Karoo National Park. Of the nearly hundred species named, every single one of them had an Afrikaans name (sometimes derived from San or Khoi words) with only a few entries in the English column.

I remember people talking about how Afrikaans names for some birds were being removed from the latest classic works on South African birds.

Is it possible that a space that has become place can revert back to space?

* * *

Groot Verseboek, believed to contain the canon of Afrikaans poetry, provides an interesting insight into how land became an indispensable root for Afrikaans poetry. After some light rhymes about drunkenness, ghosts, romance and marriage, four of the main members of Die Genootskap van Regte Afrikaners (The Fellowship of True Afrikaners) wrote what they called: 'Di Afrikaanse Folksliid' (The Afrikaans Anthem).

In the first line of the first stanza, Arnoldus Pannevis, C.P. Hoogenhout, D.F. du Toit and S.J. du Toit use the word 'land' in a rhyming position and in capitals:

'n Ider nasi het syn LAND,
Ons woon op Afrikaanse strand.

(Every nation has its country,
We live on Afrikaans beach/territory.)

I wonder how it was possible that four reasonably talented and inspired men came up with such a forced rhyme: *land/strand* instead of using words with more possibilities such as *stand* (position), *wand* (wall), or *kant* (side).

Stating that Afrikaners were living on a beach (albeit that an Afrikaans beach for them was very different from an ordinary South African beach) was conveying the opposite of the brave but embattled nation they were trying to portray. What is more, a nation living on the beach is simply skirting the edges; it means that the inside, the real *binneland* (interior), the heart of the country, does not belong to them.

But any suspicions that the word *strand* may be suggesting that Afrikaners are nothing but a group of Strandlopers (beachcombers; a colonial term for Khoi people) is sunk by the following stanzas: after 'LAND' comes 'TAAL' (language – from the Cape to Transvaal) bringing to every nation its 'LAW', its 'RIGHT' and, inevitably, its 'TIME'.

Clearly *strand* was more of a Freudian slip for the *slegs-blanke strande* (whites-only beaches) that were soon to follow from the rhyming horizons.

Land, however, was also the mark of maturity of Afrikaans as a language of literature. In his poem about land, 'Winternag' (Winter's night), Eugene Marais did not celebrate land, but lamented how *veld* – wide as the mercy of God – lying in starlight and shade – had been razed to the ground by the British troops.

Like the Basotho chief described by Casalis, Marais was conveying a story of destruction, loss and grief.

* * *

These days academics are rated according to what they publish in accredited journals. Similarly, universities and researchers are rewarded for the papers they publish in these journals. Because there is no accreditation for writing accessible pieces for a newspaper, or explaining intricate concepts in laymen's language, few academics go to the unrewarding trouble of trying to put some of their research across to ordinary readers. Consequently, very little of what is being published in accredited journals ever finds its way into everyday life. In addition, newspapers are usually unwilling to publish 'academic' material or analytical stories. And so we have a country where we can hear one another speaking of the land, but do not necessarily understand a word being said.

In this context, I am thankful that somebody as finely tuned towards South African texts as Duncan Brown has seen his way open to put a book together that is also 'usable' for ordinary readers on a quest to understand how we live with each other in this land. I am even more thankful that the University of KwaZulu-Natal Press sees its way open to publish and distribute a text that illuminates a postcolonial society in this way.

With a nose for unknown or lesser-known texts, Brown has chosen the amazingly visceral poetry of Xhosa poetess Nontsizi Mgqwetho. I had never heard of her and it was a pleasure to be introduced to her work. Brown is, and this cannot be praised enough, willing to work with translations which enables him to present, apart from Xhosa poetry, one of the rare discussions of Mazisi Kunene's *Emperor Shaka the Great.*

An instinct for texts that weave longing and belonging also enables Brown to provide a sensitive reading of the last poems of Douglas Livingstone about living and being on a peripheral and always shifting border. It is fascinating to see this chapter finding its feet in a book where texts are trying to affirm to their marginalised and formerly oppressed writers a right of place.

Brown's inclusiveness and the generous attention he has always given to the cultural nuances of KwaZulu-Natal have enriched this book immensely. His comprehensive discussion of the speech patterns found at 'the edge' of Cato Manor in the stories of Ronnie

Govender is an indication of an awareness for texts from the margins of society.

To my delight, Brown ends this book with 'rap' and Prophets of da City. Many poetry and literature lovers have big reservations about, if not downright resistance to, rap. Brown, knowing that he deals with a sceptical and 'uneducated' audience, opens with the basics: the difference between rap and hip-hop followed by detailed explanations of the culture, the rhythm, and so on, without shying away from the misogyny and racism of some of the lyrics.

* * *

After winning the Mondi Best Journalist of the Year Award in 2005, cartoonist Zapiro was a guest on a radio phone-in programme.

Zapiro's work is appreciated by many people. Every year his latest cartoon book sells in its thousands and many letters to newspapers comment on his work. But the calls coming through on the phone-lines after he had received the award were mainly from people in rural areas. One man said he was teaching ecology and using a specific Zapiro cartoon for his class. A different caller was a pastor and he had used a Zapiro cartoon to illustrate something because it got people talking. Another person had used one of the cartoons because it explained something well. It was clear that many people used the cartoons as a way of 'hearing' or 'understanding' other people, or as a way of 'discussing' issues.

Is the fact that this award, usually reserved for a journalist, went to a cartoonist not telling us something besides the fact that Zapiro is fulfilling journalistic criteria in a unique way? Is it perhaps not also saying that many things are happening in this country that we need to understand beyond the first layers of reporting?

We have had many years of telling stories: some were heard; others went underground; some were written; some were oral; some were trapped in neglected mother tongues; others went digital. Fragments of these stories are now often mirrored by the media, but they are seldom analysed and given back to us in a way that we can talk about.

We hear all these stories and so often we do not know how to understand them. This action of giving our stories back to us, analysed, is precisely the reason why this book by Duncan Brown should be coveted.

Antjie Krog
Cape Town

Bibliography

Brink, André P. 2000. *Groot Verseboek*. Kaapstad: Tafelberg.

Casalis, Eugene. 1965 [1861]. *The Basutos or Twenty-three Years in South Africa.* Cape Town: C. Struik.

Darian-Smith, Kate, Liz Gunner and Sarah Nuttall (eds.). 1996. *Text, Theory, Space: Land, Literature and History in South Africa and Australia.* London and New York: Routledge.

Introduction

The Canadian geographer Peter Usher tells of a meeting between a Native-Canadian community and a group of government foresters in the north-west of Canada about jurisdiction over the woodlands. The Native-Canadians were bemused by the claim of people whom they regarded as relative newcomers. Finally, one of them put the problem into words: 'If this is your land, where are your stories?' (Chamberlin 1998: 13).[1]

This book is concerned with the implications of this question for South African society, and those societies in analogous situations. Through a series of case studies, which range from rock painting and oral storytelling to rap music, I consider how people have, historically and in the present, used different textual forms to express, accomplish and enact a sense of what it means to live (in) a place, in terms of intimacy, ownership, usage, displacement or alienation. I do not offer a single thesis – a model according to which identity and belonging are negotiated or mediated – for the subject matter seems to militate against any kind of unitary response. Rather, I seek to develop the arguments through attention to particular material and contexts, and my approach is more implicit and suggestive. The ways in which people claim identity and belonging are various, complex and contradictory, and do not allow for simple definition or analysis: ranging from the overarchingly national to the sensually intimate; from the metaphoric to the pragmatically economic; from the habitually used to the politically declared; from the linguistically intuitive to the legally defensible;

and from the tactile to the intangible. What Homi Bhabha says of the analogous problem of trying to define nationalism may be pertinent here. He talks of:

> a form of living that is more complex than 'community'; more symbolic than 'society'; more connotative than 'country'; less patriotic than *patrie*; more rhetorical than the reason of the state; more mythological than ideology; less homogeneous than hegemony; less centred than the citizen; more collective than 'the subject'; more psychic than civility; more hybrid in the articulation of cultural differences and identifications – gender, race or class – than can be represented in any hierarchical or binary structuring of social antagonism. (1990: 291–92)

I have chosen material for discussion that I think illuminates particularly important or intriguing questions for South African society and others in postcolonial contexts. The authors and producers of the material cover a range of linguistic, racial, economic and historical contexts, but all seem to me to speak compellingly of issues that reverberate widely through present-day South Africa and beyond. An obvious omission is the extensive literature in Afrikaans dealing with questions of identity and belonging. I have deliberately avoided this area for two reasons: firstly, it has been extensively (and vigorously) discussed elsewhere; and secondly, a proper engagement with the – sometimes complicit, sometimes resistant, sometimes divided – relationship between Afrikaans narratives and poetics of place and apartheid ideology requires a far deeper understanding of Afrikaans literary history than I possess as an academic who has focused on South African English writing/performance or African-language material in English translation.

* * *

Chapter 1 of this book examines expressions of rights, ownership and belonging by Bushman/aboriginal[2] people in South Africa and elsewhere. These issues are usually debated by constitutional lawyers, or by development or environmental workers, yet it seems to me that literary and cultural studies have important contributions to make. Arguments about aboriginal identity and rights cross constantly into the fields of representation and analysis, and here the legal or scientific/environmental understandings are often inadequate. I engage with various texts and reading practices from South Africa and other countries facing the apparently conflicting demands of cultural difference and national belonging: legal judgments; nineteenth-century narratives and illustrations; rock painting; tracking; recent interviews; and creative/theoretical accounts of aboriginality and identity. I argue that, far from involving contradictions or unbridgeable divisions of knowledge or assumption, the apparently atavistic understandings of aboriginal peoples are often fundamental to modern and postmodern beliefs and practices; that aboriginal societies are often able to negotiate the divides of ancient beliefs and modern science in ways that may be illuminating for us in our present circumstances.

Chapter 2 discusses African-Christian identity in South Africa. Through an analysis of the work of the Xhosa poet, Nontsizi Mgqwetho, I consider how Christianity has become a powerfully, if not always unproblematically, indigenised form of expression and identification. Black Christianity in (South) Africa and other colonial or postcolonial contexts is often discussed in binarised terms – conversion as coerced or pragmatic capitulation to colonial/Western power/modernity versus African Christianity as a subversion of 'true' Christian doctrine. By contrast, I wish to suggest a more complex understanding of the role of African Christians in shaping a mode of speaking and belief that informs so much of historical and contemporary life in South Africa.

Chapter 3 deals with Mazisi Kunene's epic poem *Emperor Shaka the Great* (1979), and its implications for the politics of identity and place. I identify what I perceive to be the real possibilities and strengths of this poem, while acknowledging the often contradictory 'structures of feeling' that inform it. Kunene speaks from, and of, positions of conflicting local, national and global identification and allegiance that are evident in South African and African societies today – particularly in the rhetoric of citizenry and rights deployed by Thabo Mbeki – though Kunene's own position in South African/ African literary histories and scholarship remains somewhat anomalous.

Chapter 4 focuses on Douglas Livingstone's collection of poetry, *A Littoral Zone* (1991). In this volume, Livingstone undertakes a remarkable project of mapping his identity and work onto the landscape in which he lived, worked and moved: he claims belonging – in terms of mythology, molecular biology, history, relationships and literature – while acknowledging estrangement – through environmental despoliation, personal loss, history, loneliness and death. Livingstone explores these issues in ways that are at once locally specific and globally resonant.

Chapter 5 discusses Ronnie Govender's *'At the Edge' and Other Cato Manor Stories* (1996), in which he offers a series of narratives of life in Cato Manor from the 1940s until its destruction in 1958–59. Against the apartheid state's strict control of identity and space, its narrative of separation and displacement, and its official cartography of racial and economic division, Govender sets an unofficial cartography of knowing, belonging and growing, an oral-influenced mobility of storytelling, a carnival of voices, the ingenuity of survival – as well as the desolation that followed the destruction of Cato Manor and the forced removal of its residents. While the stories deal with a particular locale, they reverberate with larger claims about South African Indian identities, without essentialising or valorising them, and without constructing them as identities of exclusion or glossing over areas of difficulty or prejudice.

Chapter 6 concludes the book with an investigation of expressions of identity and belonging in South African rap music, focusing on the band Prophets of da City. My concern is with the way in which identity and locatedness are expressed, claimed and performed through lyrics, music, dance, style, and the associated activities of hip-hop culture, including graffiti or spray-can art. Engaging as a critic with performance genres always involves difficult questions of approach and methodology, but rap is a form with its own very specific challenges for criticism. It is mobile, shifting, yet with a long generic history; playful, irreverent, deeply serious; challenging and confrontational, yet often deeply conservative; finding politics in pleasure. Part of my task in this chapter, then, is to find an approach and a form to write about rap music that can balance intellectual analysis with the mobilities and pleasures of the genre itself; which can maintain the validity of academic enquiry, while subjecting the academy to challenge by voices outside of it.

The chapters are arranged chronologically to assist readers in navigating their way through subject matter that is wide-ranging and varied. There is no suggestion of teleology: that articulations of belonging develop greater complexity or compulsion in the more recent material. Indeed, the nineteenth-century narratives of //Kabbo seem to me to talk challengingly, confrontationally and sometimes supportively to those negotiating the demands of identity and belonging in the early twenty-first century.

1

Stories of Land, Land of Stories

Aboriginality, Identity and Belonging in South Africa and Beyond

Amongst the most pressing, and apparently intractable, problems facing postcolonial societies are the rights of peoples known variously as aboriginal peoples, first peoples or first nations:[1] rights to land, self-determination, natural resources, mineral deposits, the preservation of sacred sites or customs, and so on. Newspapers in South Africa and abroad feature articles on a daily or weekly basis with titles that suggest the variety of such problems and responses to them. Some examples include: 'Conservation Group Clashes with Indian Tribe over Whales' (Reed 1998); 'Dumped in a Bleak New Home, San Try to Cling to their Culture' (Herbert 1998); 'There is no Freedom in this Country' (Gabriëlse 2002); 'Battle to Find a Common Language to Give Vanishing Cultures a Voice' (Segal 1998); 'Bridge too Far for Black Australia' (Zinn 1998); 'Inuits Get their Promised Land' (Borger 1999); 'The Art of Survival through the Ages' (Gowans 2002a); 'Respect will Save Rock Art Heritage' (Gowans 2002b); 'The Trail of Tears in the United States' (Mkondo 1998); 'A Lesson in Sharing from America's First Nations' (Mitchell 1999); 'Bushmen on the Spoor to Nowhere' (Jordan 1998); 'Fat Windfall for the San' (Barnett 2002); 'De Beers Warning on San Action' (Weaver 2002); and, bizarrely, 'Cannibal Chutney a Matter of Taste' (Adams 1998).

While some claims for aboriginal rights have been successful, they are often considered – in contexts of modern democracy, global capitalism and advanced technology – to be at best atavistic, or at worst completely incommensurable with their context. In this chapter I wish to consider whether the nature of such claims, indeed the nature of the societies that make them, is so 'different' – so removed from the concerns of modernity and postmodernity – or whether there are not also important aspects of 'identity'.[2] Such a consideration may shed light not only on 'their' claims and concerns, but also on 'our' society and its often hubristic assumptions.

Some of the most visible cases about aboriginal rights have revolved around land. Probably the best-known have been the Mabo (1992) and Wik (1996) judgments in Australia. Mabo was a landmark judgment in Australian and international law which ruled that land rights existed before colonisation and continue to exist in the present – a legal principle referred to as Native Title. In making its judgment, the court rejected the notion of *terra nullius* (empty land) according to which colonial occupation and possession were often justified. The Mabo judgment paved the way for the 1993 Native Title Act in terms of which groups of Aboriginal people have been entitled to file claims for land 'on which they must prove a continuing and traditional connection' (Zinn 1998).

The 'Wik decision' – made in terms of the Native Title Act and named after the group who won a court action in 1996 – caused much consternation amongst many white Australians because of the precedent they feared it established. The Wik were evicted from their land in 1950 to make way for a 110-year mining lease, yet in a legal appeal they claimed successfully that 'native title could co-exist successfully with pastoral and mining leases' (Zinn 1998). This court decision led to such heated political debate about land rights that the 1998 election was dubbed a 'race election' – the first federal election to be fought largely on Aboriginal policy. Parliamentary debate on the issue became so bitter and rancorous that the press was banned from taking photographs in the chamber.

Such debates have their parallel in, amongst many other places, Botswana. The government there wishes to remove Bushman people from their land to extend cattle farming operations, and to reduce their hunting rights, which may be more lucratively sold to overseas tourists. In the United States, despite a brutal policy of 'terminating' tribes and 'assimilating' members, which was later officially overturned, the Native American question remains a vexed one. As Rich Mkondo points out, there are '558 nations consisting of 2.4 million people living on or near tribal land, each recognized by the US government as a sovereign entity with varying degrees of power', speaking more than 250 languages (1998). In Canada, the Inuit people have successfully lobbied for a self-governing homeland, called Nunavut; and, on a far more limited scale, in South Africa, a group of Bushmen at Kagga Kamma have been granted land rights in the area abutting the Kalahari Gemsbok Park on the grounds of traditional ownership.

Other aboriginal claims have centred on hunting rights, though these are, of course, often closely tied to land claims. For example, the International Whaling Convention has allowed the Makah Indians of Neah Bay, Washington State, who have lived in the area for at least 40 000 years, the right to hunt one grey whale a year for at least five years as part of an annual ceremony. (They have not hunted them for at least 70 years as numbers have dwindled.) This permission has been granted under the 'aboriginal subsistence' clause that exempts native people from other controls on whaling: 'The Indians' lawyers argued successfully that "subsistence" also meant cultural survival, a position supported by the US government. Yet it had an interest too: an 1855 treaty with the Makah in which, in return for thousands of ceded hectares, Washington specifically allowed them to continue whaling' (Reed 1998).

I hope to shed light on these issues by examining certain textual expressions of rights, ownership and belonging by aboriginal people in South Africa and elsewhere. These issues are usually the subjects of scrutiny by constitutional lawyers or development or environment workers, yet it seems to me that literary and cultural studies have important contributions to make. Debates about aboriginal identity cross constantly into the fields of textual representation and analysis. Here the discourses of law or scientific environmentalism often reveal shortcomings: mechanistic understandings of systems of meaning; dutiful applications of pre-given models or theories; and a lack of reflexivity. I shall engage with a variety of texts and reading practices from South Africa and other countries facing the apparently conflicting demands of cultural difference and national belonging: court cases; nineteenth-century accounts and illustrations; rock painting; tracking; recent interviews; and creative/theoretical accounts of aboriginality and identity. I shall suggest that, far from involving contradictions or unbridgeable epistemological or cognitive divides, the apparently atavistic understandings of aboriginal peoples are often fundamental to modern and postmodern beliefs and practices (including the 'unit' of modernity – the nation-state); and that aboriginal societies are often able to negotiate the divides of ancient beliefs and modern science in ways that are illuminating for us in our present circumstances. It is too often the anthropologist, the folklorist, the ethnographer and the literary scholar who lament the embracing of modern technologies or 'ways' by hunter-gatherer or indigenous peoples; who police the divides of traditional and modern – setting up, as Isabel Hofmeyr has rather acerbically put it, a 'wail for purity' (1995).

Taking the longer view, then, rather than an epistemological or cognitive break – which we might variously characterise in terms of tradition/modernity, orality/literacy, prehistory/history, custom/civilisation, and so on – we should perhaps think (without denying the enormous economic and military power behind the modernising project and its promotion of so-called Western rationality) of influences and trends that swirl together in myriad and ever-changing forms, manifesting themselves in diverse and shifting ways in the historical contingencies of human societies. In asserting aspects of 'identity', this is not to gloss over strong aspects of 'difference' that characterise, for example, nineteenth-century /Xam Bushman lives or twentieth-century Pintupi Australian Aboriginal people.

* * *

The problems of 'first nation' identity played themselves out in dramatic fashion in a court case in Canada in the late 1980s. I wish to spend some time examining the nature of the claims made and the judge's responses, since these prove illuminating both in the apparent dichotomies set up in and by the court, and in the way the case itself began to collapse (under) these dichotomies (though the judgment was unaffected).

In the case of DelgamUukw vs. the Queen (May 1987–March 1991), the Gitksan and Wet'suwet'en went to court to demonstrate jurisdiction over their ancestral territory in what is now north-western British Columbia.[3] The problem for the Gitksan and Wet'suwet'en arose over the 'organised society' test applied in such cases by courts. To assert that they have collective rights, societies must demonstrate that they have a collective history. However, in relation to aboriginal peoples, 'the court wanted proof that they not only have a continuous history, but a civilized history as well' (Chamberlin 1998: 6). This implied – in the court's definition – written historical records. Though the judge, Allan McEachern, wished initially to apply the 'hearsay' rule to render inadmissible as evidence the *ada'ox* and *kungax* oral forms of these societies, he did finally allow the performance of songs and stories in which the Gitksan and Wet'suwet'en recounted their 10 000-year history (Chamberlin 1998: 17). Judge McEachern was clearly unhappy about the violation of the decorum of his court by singing (even claiming that he had 'a tin ear'), and attempted unsuccessfully to have the songs transcribed instead for his consideration. He was finally unmoved by the performances, and dismissed the case. 'The plaintiff's ancestors had no written language, no horses or wheeled vehicles', he said. They must have 'roamed from place to place like beasts of the field' (Chamberlin 1998: 6).

The judge might, of course, have reminded himself that 'nations' with written histories rely for their creation of national feeling not so much on written texts as on oral performances – the national anthem, the oath of allegiance, or the informal 'telling' or 'quoting' of the national narrative – or on non-verbal 'texts', such as national flags and emblems. Yet these are considered no less 'true' for being in oral or symbolic form. It would be interesting, for example, to ascertain how many South Africans have actually seen, let alone read, the founding document of our new nationhood, the *Constitution of the Republic of South Africa* (1996). Again it is a curious anomaly that heraldry is an established and venerable Western cultural practice, while totemic representations, the ornamentation of spears or walking sticks and so on have only recently, and by no means universally, been recognised as sophisticated forms of cultural encoding. Judge McEachern's decision was later rejected by the Supreme Court of Canada, 'but even with the best will in the world that court was unable to find a better way of characterizing oral traditions than by saying that they were "not steeped in the same notions of social progress and evolution" as written traditions' (Chamberlin 1999: 1).[4]

The apparent epistemological and cognitive divide at the centre of the case of DelgamUukw vs. the Queen is perhaps best illustrated by the episode recounted in the Introduction, in which a group of government foresters claiming land on behalf of the state in the north-west of Canada were asked by members of the Native Canadian society: 'If this is your land, where are your stories?' (Chamberlin 1998: 13). No doubt Judge McEachern's sharp rejoinder would have been, 'If this is your land, where are your title deeds?' And yet, we should ask whether there is necessarily an unbridgeable ontological, epistemological or cognitive divide between 'stories' and title deeds, between the 'legendary' narrative and the 'document' of modernity, and if so, for whom? The evidence of the Gitksan and Wet'suwet'en suggests not for them.

As part of their performance, the Gitksan narrated a story about the spirit of the valley – a grizzly bear called Mediik – near the mountain of Stekyooden where many of them lived. The people lived so well that 'they forgot the ways that the mountains, rivers, plants and animals had taught them', the story claims (Chamberlin 1998: 23). After many warnings, the grizzly bear came storming down the mountain in a rage, bringing down an avalanche that covered the valley floor and the village of Temlaxam and killed most of the people. This was held to have occurred about 4 000 years ago, and people later moved back to the valley although life was never as good as it had been. The story of the grizzly and the valley has remained central in Gitksan history and belief:

> Today the stories of the Gitksan move out from that valley like the spokes from the centre of a wheel or children from their parents. It is the centre of their lives, the place they came from, and the place to which they return their thoughts and their thanks. Their claims to the territory around arise from the claims which the valley has on them, and the story of the grizzly and the slide confirms both claims. (Chamberlin 1998: 23–24)

Yet the Gitksan realised quite quickly that this story had little meaning for the judge, and their leader, an educated man by the name of Neil Sterrit, arranged to have geologists drill into the valley floor for clay and rock samples. Their analyses confirmed that 4 000 years ago there had indeed been an avalanche in the valley of the size, nature and location described in the story of the grizzly. As Chamberlin argues, however, in contrast to the court, which saw the scientific account as verifying the grizzly narrative:

> Neil Sterrit and the elders of the Gitksan were at pains to persuade the judge that each story was validated by the other: that neither had a monopoly on understanding what happened; that the story line of geology was framed by a narrative just as much the product of invention and discovery as the story told by their people; and that each storyteller's imagination – whether telling of tectonic plates or of grizzly outrage – was engaged with a reality that included much more than the merely human. (1998: 24)

The judge found this difficult to comprehend, though modern (and postmodern) discursive theory tends to support the Gitksan understanding.

* * *

Perhaps Judge McEachern might have been enlightened by an account that survives in transcribed and translated form by a nineteenth-century /Xam Bushman from the Northern Cape in South Africa. In a text of extraordinary scope and import, //Kabbo negotiates with ease the issues that the Canadian court found most vexing. //Kabbo's account, one of the earliest of its kind, seems to me to speak powerfully to the questions of aboriginality, modernity and belonging in both local and global contexts.

//Kabbo was a /Xam man who had been imprisoned in Cape Town for stealing a sheep. In the early 1870s, with certain other /Xam convicts, he was passed into the care of the German linguist W.H.I. Bleek and his sister-in-law Lucy Lloyd, to assist them in their project of producing a linguistic and anthropological record of /Xam culture. The Bleek and Lloyd archives, now housed in the J.W. Jagger Library at the University of Cape Town and totalling over 12 000 pages, are amongst the most valuable collections of their kind in the world. There have been various analyses of sections of the Bleek and Lloyd material, detailing the complex mythological and spiritual understandings, the intimate knowledge of the natural world, and the brutal experience of colonial intrusion expressed by //Kabbo, Dia!kwain, /Han≠kass'o and others,[5] and I do not wish to cover this ground again. Instead, I wish to examine a piece recorded shortly before //Kabbo's return home, in which he reflects upon his time with Bleek and Lloyd, and speaks of going back to his land.

'//Kabbo's Intended Return Home' – as it is entitled in *Specimens of Bushman Folklore* (1911), a published portion of the Bleek and Lloyd records – or 'What //Kabbo Said to me about his Intended Return Home to Bushmanland' – as it is entitled in the archive –

transcribed in July and August 1873, is a text of deep spiritual imbrication with the natural world, which we might see as characteristic of pre-modernity (though also of various postmodern social movements, which have adopted aspects of the world-view and cultural insignia of hunter-gatherer or 'tribal' societies[6]). Yet it is at the same time a text of extraordinary modernity. In his account of returning to Bitterpits, //Kabbo makes claims to his land – sometimes indirectly or implicitly, but at other times directly and explicitly – in a variety of ways and from apparently contradictory epistemological assumptions. Yet it is clear that he does not hold these to be contradictory, and that each carries the same weight as the other for him.

//Kabbo's account begins with the theme of storytelling as constituting identity and affirming social bonds. He laments his present position ('For, I am here; I do not obtain stories; because I do not visit, so that I might hear stories which float along'[7] [Bleek and Lloyd 1911: 301]), and longs for his return home, for the stories which 'float out from a distance' (Bleek and Lloyd 1911: 301). This understanding of stories as embodying identity, as (re)constituted in ongoing dialogue, is clearly more complex than the rather functional understanding of many anthropologists – that oral literature mediates the most pressing issues of survival. In //Kabbo's expression, identity, and storytelling, are more mobile, transcendent and yet rooted in place than such paradigms allow. The name is a wind is a story, and these – actualities rather than metaphors for //Kabbo – establish one's existence in one's place, one's co-existence with it:

> I must first sit a little, cooling my arms; that the fatigue may go out of them; because I sit. I do merely ( )[8] listen, watching for a story, which I want to hear; while I sit waiting for it; that it may float into my ear. These are those to which I am listening with all my ears; while I feel that ( ) I sit silent. I must wait (listening) behind me, while I listen along the road; while I feel that my name floats along the road; they (my

> three names) float along to my place; I will go to sit at it; ( ) that I may listening turn backwards (with my ears) to my feet's heels, on which I went; while I feel that a story is the wind. It (the story) is wont to float along to another place. Then, our names do pass through those people; ( ) while they do not perceive our bodies go along . . . The people who ( ) dwell at another place, their ear does listening go to meet the returning man's names; those with which he returns. (Bleek and Lloyd 1911: 303–05)

We should acknowledge here //Kabbo's sense that modernity does not disrupt so-called traditional understandings. In the passage above, he explained to Bleek and Lloyd that his three names which 'float along to my place' included his 'colonial' name 'Jantje'.

Having asserted his rights to the land in terms of nominality and narrative, //Kabbo goes on to claim Bitterpits in terms of heredity:

> Their place it is not; for //Kabbo's father's father's place it was. And then //Kabbo's father ( ) did possess it; when //Kabbo's father died, //Kabbo's father was the one who possessed it. And when //Kabbo's father died, //Kabbo's elder brother was the one who possessed the place; //Kabbo's elder brother died, ( ) (then) //Kabbo possessed the place. (Bleek and Lloyd 1911: 305–07)

There is no sense of //Kabbo's establishing a hierarchy of claims in his account. The rather more prosaic, or litigious, nature of this claim is neither dominant over nor subordinate to the previous claim: it stands alongside it; or perhaps, given the emphasis on name/narrative, the claim of heredity flows from the one above.

//Kabbo was a skilled hunter, fond of describing in detail the habits of animals and his own hunting practices. Following his assertion of his inherited rights to the land, he embarks upon what appears at first to be an extended digression, in which his enthusiasm for the details of the chase seems to lead him away from the theme of his return to Bitterpits:

> For, I saw a hare. I used to shoot, sending up a bustard. I put it in (to the bag) (and) brought it home. My wife would come to pluck it, at home. She ( ) boiled it in the pot; that we might drink soup. On the morrow I would hunt the hare, I would be peeping about in the shade of the bushes. I would shoot it up, that the children might eat. (Bleek and Lloyd 1911: 311)

As the account of hunting practices continues in the narrative, however, it becomes clear that //Kabbo is making a third claim to his land. In particular, his shift from the past tense of memory or habit ('I used to go . . .') to the projected future ('I shall go to drink at home') (Bleek and Lloyd 1911: 315) suggests a broader purpose to this discourse on hunting – though it may also be a narrative technique to portray vividly the hunter's feelings at the time (a shift into the interiority of characterisation and direct speech). This becomes explicit when //Kabbo names the places and features of his land, and describes the behaviour of the animals and his own hunting methods in relation to these known and named features. The land is his because he knows it as no one else does:

> The rain must first fall, and then, I should be looking around, seeking for (a pair of) ostriches which are wont to seek the water along the 'Har Rivier', ( ) that they may, going along, drink the water. I must, going round in front, descend into the 'Har Rivier'. I must (in a stooping position) steal up to them in the inside of the river bed. I must lie (on the front of my body) in the river bed; that I might shoot, lying in the river bed. For the western ostriches do, seeking water, come back; that they may, going along, ( ) drink the new water. (Bleek and Lloyd 1911: 315)

Directly after these words, //Kabbo makes claims to his land in terms of the transactional model of modernity, using the concepts of 'purchasing', literacy and the gun. None of these is perceived to invalidate the (largely 'traditional') claims made previously. //Kabbo describes his work with Bleek and Lloyd – in their own translation – as 'teaching': 'Therefore, I must sit waiting for the Sundays on which I remain here, on which I continue to teach thee' (1911: 315). The choice of this term suggests that while Bleek and Lloyd were in a position of power over their /Xam informants (//Kabbo and the others remained prisoners for much of their time with the two, and addressed Bleek and Lloyd as 'Master' and 'Mistress'), this did not necessarily involve, as in so much colonial and postcolonial theory, an internalised sense of their own inferiority. Indeed, //Kabbo seems to have a distinctly modern sense, not of barter or exchange, but of 'buying', literally of his possessing 'cultural capital' – for he wishes to purchase certain things with his knowledge: boots ('that I must put on to walk in; which are strong for the road' [Bleek and Lloyd 1911: 315]); and a gun ('Therefore, I lived with him [Bleek], that I might get a gun from him; that I might possess it' [Bleek and Lloyd 1911: 317]). //Kabbo also reveals some understanding of print and ownership – of land belonging to a person not simply because that person knows its stories or the habits of its animals, but in terms of title deeds: 'For, I shall not go to other places; for, I must remain at my own place, the name of which I have told my Master; he knows it, (having) put it down. And thus ( ) my name is plain beside it' (Bleek and Lloyd 1911: 315–17). The gun, so powerful a symbol of colonial oppression for people such as //Kabbo, is perceived to be in complete accordance with the claims made for land and identity earlier in the account (as is the wagon, or cart, in which he had previously been carried to prison, but which he hopes will now bring his firearm). For //Kabbo, the gun will enable him to hunt more effectively in changed conditions, and in old age. It will allow him to provide his share for others (Bushman groupings have defined and established procedures for sharing meat, so that all may be fed); to live his land, his identity and his inheritance fully, in the way in which he knows:

> It is there that I sit waiting for the gun; and then, he will send the gun to me there; while he sends the gun in a cart; that which running, takes me the gun. While he thinks, that I have not forgotten; that my body may be quiet, as it was when I was with him; while I feel that I shoot, feeding myself. For, starvation was that on account of which I was bound, – starvation's food, – ( ) when I starving turned back from following the sheep. Therefore, I lived with him, that I might get a gun from him; that I might possess it. That I might myself shoot, feeding myself, while I do not eat my companions' food. For, I eat my (own) game.
>
> For, a gun is that which takes care of an old man; it is that with which we kill the springbok which go through the cold (wind). We do, satisfied with food, lie down (in our huts) in the cold (wind). It (the gun) is strong against the wind. It satisfies a man with food in the very middle of the cold. (Bleek and Lloyd 1911: 317)

//Kabbo never received the gun, though it is unclear whether this was because Bleek died before he could send it (he died on 17 August 1875), or because //Kabbo himself died before it could be sent (//Kabbo died on 25 January 1876 shortly after his return to Bitterpits).

What is extraordinary about this narrative, and has prompted me to deal with it at some length, is the way in which //Kabbo is able to think across epistemological divisions that are often held to be absolute: orality/literacy; tradition/modernity; prehistory/history; barter/capital; and so on. I do not wish to deny the devastating effect of modernity on //Kabbo and his people. By 1911, the /Xam had been all but destroyed by a colonial policy best described as genocide, and I have discussed some /Xam texts in this regard elsewhere (Brown 1998). However, what concern me here are the implications of this text for understandings of the place and rights of aboriginal peoples now: //Kabbo's understandings, of 130 years ago, seem immensely illuminating today.

* * *

//Kabbo's account suggests that – like the Gitksan over 100 years later on another continent – he does not perceive his appropriation of aspects of Western technological modernity (boots, the gun, and even to a limited extent the written word) as in any way contradicting or undermining his /Xam understanding of the world.[9] //Kabbo's criterion for cultural borrowing, like Kwame Anthony Appiah's, appears to be usefulness (Appiah 1992: 157). Indeed, as I have tried to suggest in my analysis, //Kabbo's account consistently undermines the binaries of Western thought. As the Canadian court case discussed above indicates, amongst the most powerful of these binaries is that of orality and literacy, according to which theorists from Goody and Ong onwards have distinguished between 'oral' and 'literate' societies: a distinction that has provided ideological legitimation, in forms of both crude and subtle Social Darwinism, for acts of covert appropriation or outright genocide. Even the Canadian Supreme Court was unable – in the case of DelgamUukw vs. the Queen – to move beyond an evolutionist understanding of orality and literacy. Yet on closer scrutiny, the absolute distinctions set up around the orality/literacy divide prove false, and the extraordinary shortcomings and advantages arrayed on either side of this binary cannot be sustained by the claimed technological ability to make signs in or on a suitable physical surface: an ability not confined to those societies conventionally described as literate. As Chamberlin argues, it becomes clear that cultures are not themselves 'oral' or 'written'; it is merely 'that some of their most important forms of expression sometimes are' (1998: 13). With the collapsing of the orality/literacy binary, and the distinctions which flow from it, much that is held to be exclusively the preserve of modernity, or modern habits of understanding and mind, proves not to be so. In making this claim, I do not deny the extraordinary impact on the world of the printed word, and its implication in the development of nation-states and the public sphere, the institutionalisation of forms of civil governance, the development of technology, and so on – which are held to be the defining marks of modernity, and which have changed utterly the nature of the world. I am simply arguing against the hubristic assumption that such developments involve intellectual abilities which are distinct from, and superior to, those of other societies, whether in the past or socially/geographically distant. Much has been written recently to undermine such binarised and arrogant thinking, but perhaps the best refutation comes from the so-called oral societies themselves.

Bushman people, for example, may not have used alphabetic forms, but they have covered many of the rock faces of the African subcontinent with a 'script' of extraordinary beauty and complexity: their rock paintings and engravings. Recent scholarship, drawing on extensive fieldwork, comparative analyses, and dating systems, as well as historical archives such as those of Bleek and Lloyd and more recent archaeological research, suggests that Bushman rock art involves aesthetic abilities and spiritual insights at least the equal of those of contemporary Western art practice. Such debates are relatively well known, particularly through the work of writers such as David Lewis-Williams, Thomas Dowson, Patricia Vinnicombe and Anne Solomon. What is often forgotten in considering rock art, though, is the location and extent of it. There are paintings in almost every area of South Africa with suitable rock faces. Some areas, such as the southern Drakensberg, have paintings in almost every cave, on every overhang, in every crevice, in every valley (though many are now defaced or weathered). Indeed, it is hardly an exaggeration to describe the hills and mountains around Underberg, to take an area with which I am most familiar, as an extraordinary and intricate mural, of a scope and magnitude that is difficult to comprehend. Research is presently investigating the interrelationship of rock art sites across areas, suggesting that the symbolism, nature and location of paintings establish cognitive maps of place, in a way akin to Aboriginal Songlines, or //Kabbo's connection of story, name and land. What we have in this rock art is a script of belonging that uses an 'alphabet' of symbols, signs, colours, shapes and images in making its meaning, and which demands intelligent 'reading'.

This sense of Bushman people as having highly developed understandings of signification is borne out in an analogous way in the Bleek and Lloyd records. In what must have been amongst the first occasions on which a Bushman person put pencil to paper, on 4 September 1878 /Han≠kass'o drew a porcupine's hole with what are recognisably several sets of its tracks. An explanation for this picture might be that it constituted a transposition of the techniques of rock engraving or painting to the page: Dia!kwain did say 'that his father, Xaa-ttin, had himself chipped pictures of gemsbok, quaggas, ostriches, etc., at a place named !Kann, where these animals used to drink before the coming of the Boers' (Bleek and Lloyd 1911: xiv). However, particularly as /Han≠kass'o was not an engraver, we should perhaps look to another explanation for the picture. It seems likely from the nature of the illustration – with newer footprints overlaying older ones, and exits from the hole in varying directions – as well as from other information about tracking from Dia!kwain, //Kabbo and others in the Bleek and Lloyd archives, that it is no accident that /Han≠kass'o should have chosen animal tracks as the subject for his picture. For him, as for other /Xam Bushmen and for those who still live as hunter-gatherers, animal spoor is a form of writing or signification which, in a remarkable act of imaginative projection, he transferred to the page. Spoor requires decoding, involving the analysis of signs in context, the creation of hypotheses, and so on: the same cognitive processes as reading printed texts. This point is emphasised in a context far removed from that of Bushman hunter-gatherers, in Umberto Eco's remarkable novel about monastic Europe, *The Name of the Rose* (first published in 1983). William of Baskerville says of his detecting the whereabouts of a lost horse from the evidence of spoor and broken twigs: 'And so the ideas, which I was using earlier to imagine a horse I had not seen, were pure signs, as the hoofprints in the snow were signs of the idea of "horse"; and signs and the signs of signs are used only when we are lacking things' (1984: 28). But this contention about the affinities between tracking and reading requires more detailed substantiation.

In an article entitled 'Hunting, Tracking and Reading', Chamberlin says:

> My argument is quite simple. Reading comes before writing; and the cognitive advances we sometimes associate with literacy were fully evident tens of thousands of years ago, and still are today in contemporary hunter-gatherer societies. Specifically, the complex balancing of letter and spirit, or sign and meaning, which we identify with reading practices that developed from classical through medieval to Renaissance Europe, was flourishing in a very sophisticated form in the intellectual dynamics of ancient tracking in indigenous societies around the world. (1999: 1)

Chamberlin's argument is based to a large extent on Louis Liebenberg's fascinating and provocative book, *The Art of Tracking: The Origin of Science* (1990). Drawing on extensive fieldwork in the Kalahari, as well as the study of rock art and other sources from elsewhere in the world, Liebenberg distinguishes between three levels of tracking:

> Simple tracking may be regarded as following the footprints in ideal tracking conditions where the prints are easy to follow . . . . Systematic tracking involves the systematic gathering of information from signs, until a detailed indication is built up of what the animal was doing and where it was going . . . . It is a more refined form of simple tracking, and requires an ability to recognize and interpret signs in

> conditions where footprints are not obvious or easy to follow. Speculative tracking involves the creation of a working hypothesis on the basis of the initial interpretation of signs, a knowledge of animal behaviour and a knowledge of the terrain. Having built a hypothetical reconstruction of the animal's activities in their mind, the trackers then look for signs where they expect to find them . . . . (Liebenberg 1990: 29)

Liebenberg argues that whereas simple and systematic tracking are both based essentially on inductive-deductive reasoning, speculative tracking is based on hypothetico-deductive reasoning, and 'involves a fundamentally new way of thinking' (1990: 29), 'a continuous process of conjecture and refutation to deal with complex, dynamic, ever-changing variables' (1990: 45). As with reading, 'in tracking, the basic form of information is a sign' (Liebenberg 1990: 88), though far more widely construed than just footprints.[10] In fact, as Chamberlin points out, '[t]he one thing hunters know when they see a track, a spoor or a sign of the animal is that the animal is not there' (1999: 7). These signs require reading or interpretation, which is learned, for example by Bushman trackers from the Kalahari (such as those from the !Kung or Ju/'hoansi groupings), from an early age, and through an apprenticeship that is informal but nevertheless thorough.[11] Speculative tracking of this kind

> involves an interaction between the imaginative and the critical faculties, between invention and discovery, and between teleological and mechanistic explanations; that is, a constant interplay between hypotheses and the logical consequences they give rise to. It makes up for what [David] Olson calls the limitations of the writing (that is, the tracks) it is reading – the absence of illocutionary indicators, the gap between signifier and signified, the illusory quality of the meaning embodied in the language – by speculating about causes, motives and intentions. It explains the visible world

> by a postulated invisible world. It brings to bear a new understanding of the relationship between sign and cause. (Chamberlin 1999: 6)

In their 'hermeneutics' of tracking, hunters distinguish 'objective data from theory and interpretation', and continually test hypotheses against spoor evidence, rejecting or modifying those that do not stand up (Liebenberg 1990: 71). They often stop during a hunt to debate vigorously the merits of various readings (1990: 70 and throughout). Indeed, Liebenberg argues that the Bushman custom of sharing meat amongst all members of the group gives them greater licence – a kind of 'academic freedom' – to 'try out' differing interpretations (1990: 162).[12] According to Liebenberg's understanding, the skills of tracking are akin to those of much Western intellectual analysis, and he claims that the origins of science lie in tracking: that both involve the same cognitive abilities and assumptions; the same willingness to work with an hypothesis while granting its hypothetical nature. This ability of trackers to manage the 'contradictions of representation' (Chamberlin 1999: 8) fundamentally undermines any sense of absolute divisions between 'aboriginal' and 'modern' societies – between 'oral' and 'literate' humanity.

While such understandings may have significant theoretical and legal implications for societies faced with things such as 'the organised society test', they can also have more direct, local outcomes. In this respect, it is salutary to note that aboriginal societies themselves are often concerned with the pragmatics of survival over the apparently esoteric concerns of discursive representation.[13] (Though, of course, discourse shapes the policy that affects the pragmatics.) Stock theft in the Underberg region in the second half of the 1990s became so bad that – in extreme cases – farmers simply abandoned their farms in despair. In 1998, a local farmer and ex-stock theft detective, André Truter, proposed a novel solution to the problem. He had heard of the group of Bushmen at Schmidtsdrift, and the poverty and degradation in which they lived, and was also aware of the very sophisticated tracking skills which many, though not all, Bushman people (especially men), had developed. He set up a project in which – initially two, and later three – Bushman men, with their families, moved to XL farm in Underberg to assist in the recovery, through tracking, of stolen livestock. The project has been very successful.[14]

As Robert Gordon (1992) has pointed out, the myth of the pristine hunter-gatherer is one that has been used, in Namibia and Botswana, to deny Bushman peoples land and political rights – effectively to destroy them. What is significant about the Underberg project is that it does not rest on such essentialising myths. Truter has a developed sense – ironically at least partly from his knowledge of the role of the South African Defence Force (SADF) battalion of Bushman trackers in the Namibian war (the community at Schmidtsdrift comprises largely demobilised SADF soldiers and their families), though also from his own abilities as a hunter – of tracking as a skill of immense complexity, which is not innate, but *learned*. He is aware of the fact that this skill is one that survives because of a social and economic context – the life of hunting and gathering – which is rapidly disappearing. He perceives this social ability as having a new application in a context of modernity, an understanding shared by the trackers themselves. Windhoek Kamijola, Juoa Antonio and Kaskorino Viljoen, !Kung men originally from Angola, told me, in an interview that I conducted with them, about their satisfaction with their present circumstances. Whereas in Schmidtsdrift they had lived in absolute poverty and filth, with little or no prospect of employment, in Underberg they were well fed and housed, able to live with their families, and doing jobs they were good at. Like //Kabbo, who saw his request for a gun 120 years earlier as helping to establish his sense of usefulness, dignity and purpose in a changed context, they did not perceive their present circumstances as an abandonment, or contradiction, of their identity. In fact, their sense of identity remains firm – a point to which I shall return later in its more problematic aspect.

* * *

Up until this point in my argument for the undermining of binaries in understanding aboriginal societies, I have referred approvingly to the work of Chamberlin. There is, however, a more problematic aspect to his arguments, one that I think returns him unwittingly to the binaries he seeks to undermine. In considering the reluctance of Western societies to acknowledge important commonalities with aboriginal societies, he says:

> Our difficulty is a combination of ignorance and belligerence, the latter almost certainly related to an ancient antagonism between agricultural and hunter-gatherer societies. From neolithic times, the history of the world's cultures has taken shape on the imagined frontier between these two cultural forms. (Chamberlin 1999: 5)

Chamberlin correlates the agrarian/hunter-gatherer distinction with that between prose and poetry: 'the language of poetry and religion and myth provid[es] an analogue to a hunter-gatherer way of being in the world, with its typical dedication to and delight in uncertainties and indeterminacies and intractable contradictions' (1998: 7). His definition of poetry in this regard is very broad:

> In case I seem to be preoccupied with a category (the poetic) that has very narrow, perhaps even ethnocentric, associations for some readers let me hasten to add that I am using it here as a way of describing some of the apparent characteristics of hunter-gatherer languages and cultures: in which all important decisions are made by combining – and quite openly combining – intuition and deduction, dreams and reason, the oral (speech, dialogue, prayers and praise) and the written (a wide range of visual signs, both artificially and naturally produced – the traces read in tracking being one of the latter); in which there is a passionate attachment to place (hence the importance of names) but an indifference to property and for whom land – indeed territory – is at the

> centre but who don't build walls or fences or towns or cities. These cultures display apparently spectacular improvidence, and yet fierce concern for detail (like the contradictory extravagance and economy of poetry) and insistence that they know everything, and a conviction that to know everything is to know their stories and songs. (Chamberlin 1998: 9)

From this, Chamberlin goes on to argue that Western society's – or more broadly agrarian society's – rejection of the hunter-gatherer, and therefore the poetic, reflects a radical self-division or contradiction, since what is considered the Western or agrarian epitome of imaginative achievement is in fact poetic or religious language.

It is unclear on what basis Chamberlin claims this 'ancient antagonism between agricultural and hunter-gatherer societies' (1999: 5), for there are as many, if not more, examples in human history of clashes between agrarian societies. Nor is it clear why this antagonism should be related to the formal distinction between poetry and prose. It seems to me that in undermining binaries, such as those of orality and literacy, Chamberlin curiously, and unfortunately, perpetuates binarised thinking. His association of hunter-gatherers with the poetic is particularly troubling in the southern African context. Bushman peoples have long laboured under the stereotype of being 'essential poets', somehow removed from the harsh (and prosaic) concerns of survival and history. Chamberlin's argument, though he clearly does not intend this, is too close to such caricatures for comfort.

Further, if we pursue his argument using evidence from hunter-gatherer societies, it begins to collapse. Chamberlin continues from his definition of the poetic above:

> It's no wonder that the agricultural peoples of the world on all continents and of all races and creeds, the fencers and makers of landscape, the planners and producers of surplus, who weigh, measure, multiply, divide and know their friends

> and enemies and are indifferent to the rest, who seek (unsuccessfully of course) to eliminate fear in their lives while nourishing it in their art, who get stuck in their places but because their populations expand at such a rate are forever on the move to find more places to be stuck in – share an antagonism towards hunter-gatherer peoples, and to their languages. (1998: 9)

The creation and maintenance of borders, the knowing of friends and enemies, and indifference to the rest, are not restricted to agrarian peoples. Many oral literatures and other aesthetic forms from hunter-gatherer societies set up accounts of land and social groupings which include some and exclude others, establishing distinctions between those normatively 'inside' and those 'outside'. In his account of his return to his land, quoted earlier, //Kabbo defends his ownership of his land against the claims of 'strangers' in a direct and forthright manner: 'Their place it is not' (Bleek and Lloyd 1911: 305). Indeed, in his account of his arrest, he says:

> I sat beside a black man; his face was black; his mouth (was) also black; for they are black.
>
> White men are those whose faces are red, ( ) for they are handsome. The black man he is ugly, thus his mouth is black, for his face is black. (Bleek and Lloyd 1911: 299)

And //Kabbo distinguishes between various racial groups, using terms which Bleek and Lloyd translate as 'Flat Bushmen', 'Korannas', 'Kafirs', and so on. Indeed, his border management and creation of racial alterities are disturbingly close to the concerns of Bleek's own colonial ethnographic discourse, though it is unclear to what extent this is a result of //Kabbo's acculturation, the mediation of his words by Bleek and Lloyd, and/or his saying what he thought was required of him by his 'Master' and 'Mistress'. To quote a more recent example, the !Kung Bushmen living in Underberg, who had grown up as hunter-gatherers, told me that they left Namibia after independence because they did not 'wish to live with black people like Nujoma's'. In like fashion, a representative of the Bushman grouping at Kagga Kamma said:

> If I cannot live like a Bushman in my Bushman tradition, then the tradition will die out completely. And then everyone will become Basters. That time will be the end. Then I will disavow my own people, and go around stealing as well. The Basters do that! . . . If we become Basters then I will also want to be a white man. Then people will only be able to learn about the ≠Khomani in the history books. (White 1995: 20)

While I am acutely aware of the dangers of citing as evidence assertions of identity made under the influence of colonial or apartheid discourses, it seems that Chamberlin's distinction may simply be valorising. At best it may obscure some of the more problematic aspects of debates about aboriginal peoples which, painful though they may be, nevertheless demand attention. At worst it may lead us back to some hypothetical notion of purity, in terms of which any assertions of alterity or border management by hunter-gatherer societies are rejected as outside influences, because of the a priori assumption of a 'poetic' view of life and language.

Chamberlin's argument is in many ways analogous to that in one of the best-known, if also controversial, attempts to deal with the question of 'first nations', identity and land: Bruce Chatwin's *The Songlines* (first published in 1987). This text is described on its flyleaf as a 'novel of ideas', a phrase that Chatwin finally convinced his publishers to accept despite their preference for the designation 'non-fiction'. *The Songlines* follows the formal model of the French eighteenth-century dialogue novel, which Chatwin felt provided a way of 'expressing serious concepts very lightly indeed' (Murray 1993: 89–90). Despite the apparent differences between the genres of Chatwin's and Chamberlin's texts – the novel of ideas and the academic article – there are many formal similarities, especially in

Chamberlin's overt use of the devices and techniques of storytelling in his article, and in Chatwin's pursuit of a 'thesis' in his novel. *The Songlines* is a work of extraordinary scope and imaginative grasp, recounting Chatwin's attempts to understand what 'are known to Europeans as "Dreaming-tracks" or "Songlines"; to the Aboriginals as the "Footprints of the Ancestors" or the "Way of the Law"' (1988: 2). While there has been some heated debate about Chatwin's text in Australia,[15] I would argue that *The Songlines* substantially extends understandings of the nature and extent of the implication of aboriginal identity with the land:

> He [Arkady] went on to explain how each totemic ancestor, while travelling through the country, was thought to have scattered a trail of words and musical notes along the line of his footprints, and how these Dreaming-tracks lay over the land as 'ways' of communication between the most far-flung tribes . . . In theory, at least, the whole of Australia could be read as a musical score. There was hardly a rock or creek in the country that could not or had not been sung. (Chatwin 1988: 13)

These songs need continually to be performed to maintain the original Creation: 'In Aboriginal belief, an unsung land is a dead land: since, if the songs are forgotten, the land itself will die' (1988: 52). Chatwin also undermines any absolute sense of oral/literate divisions, both by portraying the extraordinary textual complexity of Dreamings, and by suggesting the interrelationship of various forms of 'scripting' and oral performance, including drawings in sand:

> [T]he Aboriginal mother makes drawings in the sand to illustrate the wanderings of the Dreamtime heroes.
>
> She tells her tale in a patter of staccato bursts and, at the same time, traces the Ancestor's 'footprints' by running her first and second fingers, one after the other, in a double

> dotted line along the ground. She erases each scene with the palm of her hand and, finally, makes a circle with a line passing through it – something like a capital Q.
>
> This marks the spot where the Ancestor, exhausted by the labours of Creation, has gone 'back in'.
>
> The sand drawings done for children are but sketches or 'open versions' of *real* drawings representing the *real* Ancestors, which are only done at secret ceremonies and must only be seen by initiates. (1988: 21–22)

Chatwin also points to the reliance of each Dreaming on an inscribed tablet known as a *tjuringa*: 'It is both musical score and mythological guide to the Ancestor's travels. It is the actual body of the Ancestor . . . . It is a man's *alter ego*; his soul . . . his title-deed to country; his passport and his ticket "back in"' (1988: 286).

Yet a problem arises with Chatwin's marshalling of this evidence in support of his thesis – similar to Chamberlin's – that nomadism is the 'natural' and 'poetic' state of humankind. He claims that his central, in fact autobiographical, concern is with 'the question of questions: the nature of human restlessness' (1988: 61): 'One day, Aunt Ruth told me our surname had once been "Chettewynde", which meant "the winding path" in Anglo-Saxon; and the suggestion took root in my head that poetry, my own name and the road were, all three, mysteriously connected' (1988: 9). He quotes J.G. Hamann, approvingly, that 'Poetry is the mother tongue of the human race as the garden is older than the field, painting than writing, singing than declaiming, parables than inferences, bartering than commerce . . .' (Chatwin 1988: 269), and draws supporting examples, as well as from Aboriginal Songlines, from such diverse sources as European 'gypsies', Arab societies, Bushmen, Greek mythology, Western philosophy, European modernism, Buddhism, Indian philosophy, the Romantic poets, Herodotus, the Bible, Darwin, modern anthropology and archaeology, and Cicero. 'The more I read', Chatwin claims, 'the more convinced I became that nomads had been the crankhandle of history' (1988: 19). However, what exactly he means by the condition of 'nomadism' is unclear, and there is a semantic slippage in his text between the terms 'nomad', 'pastoralist' and 'hunter-gatherer', which confuses rather than elucidates the argument. At times it appears that this argument relates simply to people who live 'on the move', but at other times he seems specifically concerned with pastoralists who live a mobile life of herding, though the aboriginal peoples he discusses at length are/were largely hunter-gatherers. And at yet other times his claims for a mobile, poetic existence relate specifically (and sometimes, it seems, exclusively) to 'hunters'.[16]

As well as being confused, Chatwin's argument becomes rather fanciful in its conclusions. From his consideration of developments in modern archaeology, he posits the possible existence of a 'super predator', which represents the mythical 'beast' within all human consciousness: 'Could it be, one is tempted to ask, that Dinofelis was Our Beast? A Beast set aside from all the other Avatars of Hell? The Arch-Enemy who stalked us, stealthily and cunningly, wherever we went? But whom, in the end, we got the better of?' (1988: 253). And he wishes to draw universal, and enormous, conclusions from his consideration of Aboriginal Dreaming:

> I have a vision of the Songlines stretching across the continents and ages; that wherever men have trodden they have left a trail of song (of which we may, now and then, catch an echo); and that these trails must reach back, in time and space, to an isolated pocket in the African savannah, where the First Man opening his mouth in defiance of the terrors that surrounded him, shouted the opening stanza of the World Song, 'I AM!' (Chatwin 1988: 280)

The point is simply that, as with Chamberlin's conception of poetic hunter-gatherers, Chatwin's vision, though undeniably seductive, rests on a selective and largely metaphoric understanding of human history: it sets up symbolic polarities that few human societies, engaged with the mess of the actual, can ever sustain. In

The Songlines Chatwin consistently refuses to romanticise Aboriginal peoples, yet the abstract symmetry of his own argument constantly threatens to undermine his own rigorous, and frank, engagement with his subject matter.

* * *

In an illuminating moment in *The Songlines*, Chatwin narrates an occasion on which an Aboriginal leader, Alan, considers a map with Arkady,[17] a development worker assisting Aboriginal peoples in mapping Dreamsites to protect them from damage by railroad or construction companies:

> Alan looked on with the composure of a general at a staff meeting. From time to time, he would stretch a questioning finger to some feature on the map, and then withdraw it.
>
> I mistook this performance for a charade: it never dawned on me the old man could map-read. But then he splayed both first and second fingers into a V and ran them up and down the sheet, like dividers, his lips working silently, at speed. He was, as Arkady told me later, measuring off a Songline. (Chatwin 1988: 100)

Like //Kabbo with his various – and in his view equivalent – claims to his land, or the Gitksan with their stories of grizzly bears and geology, Alan is presented as being quite able to work across the so-called epistemological and cognitive divisions of tradition and modernity, the spiritual and the scientific, the spoken and the written: to measure off a Songline on a map.

At this point we return to the question of by whom, and in whose interests, such divisions are maintained and policed. As I have argued, academia has much to answer for. While the claims of aboriginal societies are so often perceived simply as problems, in fact they represent important possibilities: the highly mobile, developed and complex insights of such societies, which often exhibit considerable spiritual and intellectual latitude, have much to teach so-called Western society, have much in common with it, and epitomise much that is central, but repressed or latent, within it. In our quest for economic development, agricultural productivity and technological sophistication, we should not lose sight of imaginative projections or spiritual complications, imbrications and attachments, which are powerfully evident in aboriginal articulations of land and landscape, but are in fact at the centre of human thought and belief – whether in the 'particle tracks' of modern science, the 'faith' of Christianity or Islam, or the creation songs of //Kabbo, Pintupi Aboriginals, or the Gitksan and Wet'suwet'en.

2

My Pen is the Tongue of a Skilful Poet

African-Christian Identity and the Poetry of Nontsizi Mgqwetho

Benedict Anderson speaks of the importance of national anthems in creating a sense of communal belonging in the nation-state: they 'provide occasions for unisonality, for the echoed physical realisation of the imagined community' (1991: 145). In South Africa, national identity is expressed and affirmed – at international sporting events, in parliament, in schools and colleges – by the singing of an anthem that opens with, and some would argue is effectively defined as, '*Nkosi Sikelel' iAfrika*' (God Bless Africa), the Christian hymn composed by Enoch Sontonga in 1897. From its performance at the launch of the South African Native National Congress (later to become the African National Congress) in 1912, this seemingly apolitical and innocuous hymn became an expression of commitment and solidarity within the anti-apartheid struggle. It is generally accompanied in its singing by a clenched fist salute, and it serves in varying forms as the national anthem of Zimbabwe, Zambia and Tanzania. Clearly – as scholars from several disciplines, including oral studies, have demonstrated – the performance of a text such as a song can come to have significance, subversive or otherwise, which seems unrelated to the apparent meaning of the lyrics.[1] But the African-Christian voice of '*Nkosi Sikelel' iAfrika*' resonates through public discourse in past and present South African society. Unlike the Bushman/aboriginal expressions of identity and belonging discussed in Chapter 1, which are often perceived as marginal, problematic or atavistic, non-Western Christian discourse is prominent and pervasive in South Africa and many other postcolonial societies.

In this chapter I investigate, in relation to the work of the Xhosa poet, Nontsizi Mgqwetho, how Christianity has become a powerfully, if not always unproblematically, indigenised form of expression and identification.[2] My concern is to move beyond the often binarised discussion of black Christianity in (South) Africa and other colonial or postcolonial contexts – conversion as coerced or pragmatic capitulation to colonial/Western power/modernity versus African Christianity as a subversion of 'true' Christian doctrine – to a more complex understanding of the role of African Christians in shaping a mode of speaking and belief that informs so much of historical and current life in South Africa, whether in the public oratory of Nelson Mandela, Thabo Mbeki and the Truth and Reconciliation Commission,[3] or in the everyday speech of millions in homes, taxi ranks, schools and places of work.

The statistics are intriguing. South Africa's population is, according to the 2001 census, 79.6% Christian.[4] As Richard Elphick points out, 'over the twentieth century Christianity has grown most dramatically among Africans . . . up from 26% of Africans in 1911 to 76% in 1990' (1997b: 1); '[b]y the 1990s few places in the world, apart from the United States, matched South Africa in the proliferation of Christian denominations and sects' (1997b: 7). Christianity has pervaded almost all aspects of South African personal and political life:

> Starting with the missionary campaign to Christianise African societies, some of the most intimate matters of white and black culture in South Africa – initiation, marriage, divorce, sexuality, association with people of other races, and even dress and drinking patterns – have been debated at length and with passion, largely in Christian terms. Also, until the 1950s, churches and missions controlled almost all schools

> for Africans and, to this day, many private schools for the largely white elite. So, too, social work, medicine, and nursing all were, to varying degrees, sponsored by Christian missions and churches. And the literature of Afrikaners and Africans was, until the Second World War, largely shaped by churches, missions, and publishers with Christian agendas; both literatures, like that of English-speaking whites, were replete with Christian motifs and allusions. (Elphick 1997b: 1)

Despite the fact that Christianity is deeply implicated in the narratives of South African life, it has until recently been inadequately reflected in South African historiography, 'whose liberal and Marxist historians, long preoccupied with the struggle between black and white, have tended to assign in this dynamic only marginal roles to religion' (Elphick 1997b: 2). Where it has been discussed, it has generally been seen as an instrument of European domination, 'a colonisation of consciousness'.[5] Yet its adoption by African people has been far more complex, nuanced, contradictory and often enabling than this historiography suggests.

The inadequate or dismissive treatment of Christianity in South African literary and cultural studies points also to a more fundamental theoretical question. In considering 'Gandhi's apparent absence from the foreground of postcolonial theory', Robert Young suggests as a reason Gandhi's 'unfashionable adherence to the "spiritualisation of politics" – the idea that the spiritual diffuses all aspects of everyday life, including the political, and should form the basis of the way humans live' (2001: 337). This, Young claims, is symptomatic of a deeper-rooted paradigmatic problem within postcolonial studies:

> Gandhi's anomalous position brings out the extent to which, as a result of its Marxist orientation, an absolute division between the material and the spiritual operates within postcolonial studies, emphasising the degree to which the field is distinguished by an unmediated secularism, opposed to

> and consistently excluding the religions that have taken on the political identity of providing alternative value-systems to those of the west – broadly speaking, Islam and Hinduism. Postcolonial theory, despite its espousal of subaltern resistance, scarcely values subaltern resistance that does not operate according to its own secular terms (Chakrabarty 2000). (Young 2001: 337–38)

While Young includes only Islam and Hinduism as providing 'alternative value-systems to those of the west' there is abundant evidence of other religions, especially in the South African context various forms of indigenised Christianity, expressing 'subaltern' concerns. Young's own study, besides identifying the lacuna, does little itself to move beyond the paradigmatic problems that it identifies. More suggestive in this regard is Dipesh Chakrabarty's study *Provincialising Europe: Postcolonial Thought and Historical Difference* (2000), cited by Young himself, which seeks amongst other things to theorise the crucial spiritual dimension of the postcolonial public sphere.

In discussing the spread of Christian ideas and beliefs in South Africa, particularly amongst Africans, and in redirecting attention to the agency of African Christians in social and cultural history, we approach the question of why Christianity has been such a potent force in our context (and others like it). Interestingly, most early white missions were spectacularly unsuccessful in terms of producing converts, and the spread of Christian belief was largely due to black evangelists. Christians might claim that it is the 'truth' of the belief which accounts for its influence – though in terms of the gap between the theology and liturgical practices of many black and white churches, it is sometimes unclear what 'truth' they agree upon. In contrast, materialist scholars would point to Christianity as discursive sanction for the economic and political rapacity of European occupation, and attribute its adoption by the colonised to coercion or hegemony. My concern is – through the work of Mgqwetho – to consider how Christianity becomes a mode of spiritual power and personal articulation for African Christians. I shall argue that she (like so many African Christians) finds in it something that the two positions above do not allow – something that undermines the pervasive, but fallacious, assumption that Christianity is a 'Western' religion. Clearly much of its ecclesiastical history has been shaped by and has shaped European history, but its origins, and its originary text(s), are in fact Middle-Eastern, and the forming biblical contexts would be comfortingly familiar to most colonial and postcolonial scholars. Some of the largest and most influential Christian communities utilise biblical exegeses and liturgical forms far removed from the maternal or avuncular orthodoxies of Catholicism or Protestantism (though their origins sometimes lie in the missionary enterprises of these churches).[6] The question is, then, whether the Bible and biblical discourse have a particular valency in 'non-Western' contexts: that, for example, African-Christian modes of belief and identity, which have been strongly evident in this country and across the continent in various forms, reflect neither the simple binary of colonial capitulation/negotiation nor heretical Christianity, but a powerful confluence of cultural and spiritual modes of being, ironically perhaps closer to originary Christianity than the beliefs and practices of the missionaries who often condemned such forms.

This is not to deny the enormous, and often brutal, power behind the biblical message in the colonial context, nor to suggest that such a confluence did not often cause profound difficulty for African Christians. There is ample evidence, in the poetry of Mgqwetho as well as in other African-Christian texts, to the contrary. It is, however, to take seriously a mode of belief and being that has influenced so many people in our country's history.

* * *

Nontsizi Mgqwetho was a Xhosa Christian poet who published between 1920 and 1929 in the newspaper *Umteteli wa Bantu* (The People's Spokesman). She is one of the first black woman poets to have produced a substantial body of work: ninety-five poems and three articles appeared between 23 October 1920 and 4 September 1926, and two more poems appeared after a two-year gap on 22 December 1928 and 5 January 1929 respectively. Jeff Opland, who has been the only critic to write on Mgqwetho (besides a brief discussion by Deborah Gaitskell in an article on women's prayer groups [1997], and an even briefer mention in Hofmeyr [2004]), says:

> Fearless, outspoken, committed, pious, anguished and often despairing, Nontsizi Mgqwetho eloquently articulates in her passionate poetry the political and social aspirations of black South Africans in the 1920s, and their bitter frustrations. A line that recurs in her poetry, punning on her own name, reads '*Hayi usizi kwizwe lenu, Nontsizi!*' (Ah, the grief that seizes your country, Nontsizi!). (Opland 2005: 3)

Other than individual poems in anthologies,[7] her work has not been republished, and I am extremely grateful to Opland for granting me access to the working manuscript in which he has collected and translated all of Mgqwetho's known works.

Opland says little in the Introduction to his manuscript about his translation strategies, besides commenting at one point that he has used the same English formulation for phrases or stanzas which reappear in different poems (there are some comments about translation in relation to specific poems in the notes, though). As a range of scholars from translation studies and other disciplines have argued, translation always involves crucial interpretive choices on the part of the translator, which fundamentally affect the transaction of meaning between source and target language texts. Opland's reticence on this subject is disappointing, particularly in light of the evidence that he himself cites of Mgqwetho's own sensitivity to the question of biblical translation. In a letter to a newspaper in 1897 she

> criticised a recent Bible revision for its flat style; rather [she] concluded, content and style should be unified, like the words and music of a song: *Ukufaka amazwi angaqelekileyo kwinteto enjenge Sibhalo, kunjengokutya ukutya okumnandi ze kugalelwe intanga ezirwada zomxoxozi, ungade uhlute ungeka qondi ukuba usesitubeni sokuhluta*, To include unfamiliar words in a text like the scriptures is like eating tasty food mixed with raw melon seeds: you feel full without quite understanding why. (*Imvo zabaNtsundu* 14 October 1897 in Opland 2005)

In personal discussions, Opland has indicated to me that he has sought, in his most recent translations, to find English verbal equivalents for Mgqwetho's assonantal and alliterative style. While the impulse is understandable, it can also present problems in terms of English idiom. To illustrate, the Xhosa stanza below is translated as follows in Opland's 1998 study *Xhosa Poets and Poetry*, with an apparent emphasis on sense and readability:

Wugqwethele Mgqwetho lo mhlaba kaPhalo
Betha izizwe ngesithunzi zidangale
Ulirhamncwa akuvelwa ngasemva
Nabakwaziyo babetha besothuka.[8]

Upset Phalo's land, Mgqwetho,
Loom over nations and sap their strength.
Wild beast too vicious to take from behind,
Your associates tremble in tackling you. (1998: 201)

A note qualifies the translation: 'Here, and elsewhere, Mgqwetho evidences verbal dexterity as she juxtaposes her name and the verb *ukugqwetha* ["to turn something upside down, to transform it"]. Paronomasia is a marked feature of *izibongo*.' The most recent manuscript translation is rather different, perhaps seeking greater fidelity to the Xhosa original, but in my opinion producing a less readable English version:[9]

Plead for Phalo's land, Mgqwetho,
whack nations till tapeworms flee.
Wild beast too fierce to take from behind,
the well-informed tremble in tackling you. (12/1/1924)[10]

Nevertheless, throughout this chapter I have used Opland's most recent translations.

The insubstantial sketch we have of Mgqwetho's life is based largely on her writings.[11] In a poem about the death of her mother, published on 2 December 1922, she gives her mother's name as Emmah Jane Mgqwetto, daughter of Zingelwa of the Cwerha clan, and associates her with the Hewu district near Queenstown. Abner Nyamende, who discussed the translation of the poems with Opland, claims that there are Moravian liturgical influences in her poetry, which may suggest that she was educated in the Eastern Cape by the Moravians, probably at Shiloh which is in the Hewu district. She seems to have lived at Peddie, possibly at Tamara, as she is – according to Opland – the likely author of two prose contributions to the King William's Town newspaper *Imvo zabaNtsundu* (Black People's Opinion) on 20 May and 14 October 1897, both signed with her clan name Cizama, and the later contribution coming from Tamara. In a poem that appeared in *Umteteli wa Bantu* on 18 December 1920 she criticises L.T. Mvabaza, editor of the newspaper *Abantu-Batho* (People), for bragging that he had brought her from Peddie to Johannesburg. Her first poem in *Umteteli wa Bantu,* published on 23 October 1920, was signed with her clan name Cizama, and sent from Crown Mines in Johannesburg. From a reference to herself in a poem,

ungainly girl with ill-shaped frame.
Oh Nontsizi, African lichen,
with bow-legs like yours you'll never marry! (12/1/1924),

it is possible that she may have been unmarried, although the hyperbolic and intertextual nature of Xhosa personal praises means that such references may not be literally 'true'. Her poems suggest that she was socially and politically active, though critical of the African National Congress (ANC) for what she perceived to be its role in dividing black opposition. She defended and promoted the first editor of *Umteteli wa Bantu*, Marshall Maxeke, and his wife, civil rights activist Charlotte Maxeke; appears to have been arrested for political activity ('I blundered in going to whites:/Oh I felt the cops' cuffs on me!' [12/1/1924]); and took part in the April 1919 demonstration against passes in Johannesburg (referred to in a prose contribution published on 13 December 1924). She was a firm supporter, as well as probably a member, of a women's prayer group, as well as active in the temperance movement.

* * *

Umteteli wa Bantu was a newspaper publishing material in a variety of languages including English, Xhosa and Sesotho. It became 'a major vehicle for Xhosa literature' (Opland 1998: 196), and carried regular contributions from, amongst others, S.E.K. Mqhayi (under the pseudonym Nzululwazi). Opland has discussed in great detail the role of newspapers in the development of Xhosa literature (1983: 201–11; 1997: 305–06; 1998: 223–61). My concern here is to consider how Mgqwetho uses the medium of newspaper publication to give voice to a committed African Christianity.

Mgqwetho was powerfully aware of the importance of the printed word in the context of early twentieth-century South Africa. In a poem on 14 March 1925, she says: 'The fingers' inscription proclaims/your country's been taken, handed to others.' Her first poem begins with a salute to the editor, Marshall Maxeke, for granting black people a medium of expression:

> Sir, Editor of our *Umteteli*,
> long life to you,
> grandson of heroes who fell at Hoho (23/10/1920);

and she often opens her poems with thanks for the 'Poets' Column' in which she publishes. But she is also very explicitly a Xhosa woman *imbongi*, as she indicates in a poem on 12 January 1924:

> LISTEN, COMPATRIOTS!
> *I sent Christmas, the old year and the new year packing with praise poems. Now I'm going to sing my own praises, and then I'll move on again to start something new. Peace to you all!*
>
> Mercy, Nontsizi, renowned for your chanting,
> your poems are the nation's bounty.
> No elephant finds its own trunk clumsy.
> Oh mercy, sheltering wing of Africa!

In the absence of biographical information, it is difficult to say with certainty whether or not 'chanting' refers to actual performance. However, as I shall argue, it is clear that, regardless of whether or not she ever performed, Mgqwetho creates a compelling form of oral address in the context, not of the Xhosa ruler's court, but of a crucial medium of what Habermas (1962) defined as the 'public sphere' of modernity and the nation-state: the printed newspaper.

The poems are complex in form. In one sense they are very obviously praise poems: they are largely non-narrative; comprise series of epithets and images about their subjects; and offer commendation, advice and criticism:

> Browsing elephant hemmed in by fences,
> Africa, speak while your people yet live.
> If whites have a fit, well then let them die:
> they thought you a low yielding cow. (28/6/1924)

In a prose contribution to *Umteteli wa Bantu* Mgqwetho said on 13 December 1924: 'It's now six years and two months since I exploded on the scene as a poet singing praises to Africa . . .'[12]; and she constantly uses the terms '*imbongi*' (praise poet), '*bonga*' (to praise) and '*izibongo*' (praises/praise poems) to refer to what she is and does. She repeats the customary tropes of praise poetry from one poem to the next, such as 'something stinks like the river snake, fouling the air' or the 'shade-screened leopard'; she draws on the praises of important Xhosa rulers; and her poems often begin and conclude with opening and closing formulae. Even as they frequently refer to their status as newspaper publications, the poems convey in print a strong rhetorical sense of the presence of the *imbongi*:

> I'll roar returning to where I began,
> I came when they said I'd come,
> babes at the breast even swear by me,
> kings stamp and prance in the yards. (26/12/1925);

or:

> Oh! Vaaibom's flamingo's had her say.
> She's not one to sip from shallow pools
> in fear of speaking out. (19/1/1924)

The poems also evoke an audience that is imagined to be present: 'Listen then! Are you one of the twelve? Are you? And you?' (10/7/1926); or

> Look! Today I want you to understand
> the essence of our distress.
> Compatriot, wrestle with what I say . . . (2/2/1924).

Iimbongi have historically always been male, and an important aspect of Mgqwetho's adaptation of the form of *izibongo* in *Umteteli wa Bantu* is her claiming the right for herself as a woman to address and admonish her society as a praise poet. In her very first poem she talks explicitly about this:

Go, we'll follow you:
no female poet
came from our house:
the poet who rouses the court
and censures the king's always male. (23/10/1920)

In another poem published shortly afterwards she points to the resistance she faces, as well as to her own determination to keep speaking:

Hen screening her chicks
safe from the grasp of birds of prey,
the nation knows you, sky-python,
poets sneer but discuss you. (12/1/1924)

Mgqwetho's tone is often ironically dismissive of the criticisms that she faces from men, and she employs humour – both self-deprecating and satirically ironic – in her responses. This humour is part of the licence of the form of *izibongo*, but Mgqwetho exploits particularly the artful manipulation of words and perceptions that is often associated with the *imbongi* to open up space for women's speech. There are several references (akin to those of the Xhosa poet David Yali-Manisi[13]) about poets being troublesome and untrustworthy, in particular the repeated refrain, 'nitpicking poets/ignore the grain that pecks the chicken' (27/9/1924, 21/2/1925 and 24/4/1926). These are poetic rather than referential statements that open rhetorical spaces for new or oppositional modes of speaking. While the mode may not be solemn, it is clearly serious, as Mgqwetho indicates in a symbolic description of her poetic address: 'So say I, who fights armed with lightning alone!' (27/9/1924). She further expands this rhetorical space for herself in the historically male domain of *izibongo* by varying the gender in which she speaks. At times she clearly identifies herself as a woman, as in the concluding line, 'Oh, the passionate woman's had her say!' (26/1/1924) and the examples quoted above, but in other situations she poses as a young man, speaking ironically of his lack of skill: 'Editor, thanks for the poets' column. I'm still here, a young man, and no poet. I was born only yesterday across the Orange River. I look old with a beard, like Hili' (28/2/1925).

As well as being *izibongo*, Mgqwetho's poems are very clearly influenced by and expressive of Christianity. As Isabel Hofmeyr has noted, in contrast to the conventional perception that the literate culture of the missionaries and the colonial enterprise simply overwhelmed oral culture, orality had a profound influence on print culture:

> In the initial confrontation of orality and literacy, it is, in fact, the former which transforms the latter, rather than the other way round, as common-sense wisdom would lead us to anticipate. In this process of transformation, a predominantly literate religion . . . becomes 'oralised' in its confrontation with African society, so that instead of becoming a religion of the printed word, it becomes a religion of the image and the spoken word. (1993: 14)

African Christians have tended to emphasise the Old Testament and its oral aspects, such as the Psalms, the oral histories of the books of Exodus, Kings and the prophets, or the sermonising/evangelising rhythms of the gospels and the book of Acts. Many of Mgqwetho's poems, like the hymns of her Zulu contemporary Isaiah Shembe, are really indigenised Psalms, in the tradition of the nineteenth-century Xhosa prophet Ntsikana:

> Who would know that greatness in you,
> Maker of heaven and earth,
> in you who made the stars and moon,
> in you who made the day and moon? (1/5/1926);

or they are praise poems to God:

You are the You who dwells on high,
cast out the heathen gods,
You're the Great God of heaven,
walking past the white man's cannon.

You are the You, the Shield of Truth,
with you, Shield of Truth, we'll guard ourselves.
You are the Truth, Fort of Truth,
Truth strengthens us in your fort. (4/10/1924)

But Mgqwetho also uses aspects of the print tradition. The poems all have titles; almost invariably they have a regular four-line stanzaic structure like that of many hymns; they have a regular length (either about fifty or eighty lines long); and many contain or refer to biblical verses. Although Mgqwetho's first 31 poems utilise the somewhat irregular and performative rhythms of *izibongo*, the final 66 move towards the regular rhyme and syllabic metre of the Western print tradition. Opland is critical of this shift, and in his translations attempts to register the movement to rhythm and metre in only the poem which marks the transition. He comments:

> This is an unfortunate development, not only because rhyme is not a feature of Xhosa tradition – and thus represents a significant departure from the poetic diction of the *imbongi* – but also because rhyme is a feature of the European culture [Mgqwetho] is elsewhere at pains to denigrate. (1998: 203)

The use of rhyme and syllabic metre in African languages has been fiercely debated, and I do not wish to engage with this question here.[14] I would, however, argue that Mgqwetho's use of these devices, successful or not, represents not the kind of departure or lapse that Opland suggests, but her continued attempts to accommodate the form of *izibongo* to new media. As she says in another poem: 'we modern poets don't lounge about:/dogs will devour you on our turf' (5/1/1924).

This accommodation is evident in the very nature of the address that Mgqwetho makes in *Umteteli wa Bantu*. In their repeated themes and images, and their formulaic modes of address, the poems seem to have the status less of individual texts – though there is an aspect of that – than of a series of addresses that draws power from the cultural authority of the institution of *izibongo*, as well as from the moral and spiritual assurance of faith and the public sphere of modernity. Many of the poems are connected to specific dates such as New Year or religious festivals such as Christmas or Easter, which provide the theme, but also crucially constitute occasions on which poetry needs to be heard (as the *imbongi* would punctuate important events with his performance).[15] In this sense the poems are interventions at a point, which usefully draw on the shared cultural signifiers of their society. While it is assumed that poems published in volumes or anthologies exist over time and will be read and reread, it seems that Mgqwetho finds a powerful congruence between the oral and newsprint modes: that like an oral poem, which generally exists only in its moment of performance, the newspaper poem will be read once and then discarded with the rest of the publication. So for Mgqwetho, the Christian *imbongi* of *Umteteli wa Bantu*, each poem assumes those that preceded it and will follow it, as well as the institution of praising itself, but it is crucially a specific address for that particular moment.

* * *

Mgqwetho is an outspoken critic of state oppression, particularly the removal of black people from their land in terms of the Native Land Act of 1913. Lines such as the following recur from poem to poem:

> Today you're a stranger in Africa,
> you go about clutching at straws:
> groom your shield, this land of your fathers
> is now the playground of strangers. (14/6/1924);

or:

We perch like birds on branches:
why are the houses of Africans burning?
Even a polecat growls in its lair
but a black has nowhere to stay. (31/5/1924)

She speaks memorably of the conditions in which she lives as being so tough that they would 'snap fencing wire', and also of the economic subordination of her people: 'we're a ladder others ascend' (14/6/1924). Her concern is particularly with the plight of African workers, and her workerist poetry foreshadows that of Alfred Qabula, Mi S'dumo Hlatshwayo and Nise Malange in the 1980s:

Unity, black workers!
I lack clay and grease to shape it.
Hurry up: see eye to eye,
clear the scrub and we'll move on together.

The courts of law have torn to shreds
the colour bar for workers.
The stench is a spearcast enticing
black nations to come together. (16/2/1924)

Her frame of reference in these workerist *izibongo* is explicitly Christian:

We must stand as one
    to face the bosses,
    lions that stalk us
    with bloody eyes.

God won't deign
    to grant us help
    unless we strive
    to help ourselves. (15/1/1921)

In addition to Mgqwetho's outspoken political opposition to white oppression, she was critical of, and faced criticism from within, the ANC.

Umteteli wa Bantu was established in 1920 by the Native Printing and Publishing Company, under the direction of the Native Recruiting Company,[16] apparently to counter the ANC's official mouthpiece *Abantu Batho*. T.D. Mweli Skota, himself an editor of *Abantu Batho*, wrote in 1931 of *Umteteli wa Bantu*: 'While it has been denounced by some as a European-controlled paper, it is certainly read by the race leaders and other progressive men in South Africa' (1931: 441). From the outset Mgqwetho defended the editor, Marshall Maxeke, and his wife Charlotte against charges of collusion with whites. She uses particularly the conventional image of the 'ford' – a suitable place to cross a river, but also a way of proceeding – to refer to the problems black people have in finding a way forward:

> We stumbled in starting!
> We seek a ford,
> a long rope for hauling
> the lame as well.
>
> The slope is benighted,
> we seek a ford:
> our fathers abandoned us,
> a flock with no kindling. (13/11/1920)

And she comments on the fact that Marshall Maxeke can provide the appropriate vision and leadership:

> Behold the risen star;
> let it alight on Maxeke, B.A.,
> the only man who knows the fords. (5/1/1924)

In contrast, L.T. Mvabaza, editor of *Abantu Batho*, is treated with derision:

Hawuleleh! Huleh!
Abantu Batho,
you thought you'd retain
the title of guardian.

Umteteli wabantu
long saw through you:
you're a waterless sack
left to breed tadpoles. (18/12/1920)

Mgqwetho's opposition to the ANC and *Abantu Batho* appears to be less ideological or spiritual than tactical. She perceives them as ineffective:

Take the African National Congress:
we once burst our ribs in its praise.
Now we go round in search of it:
'Has anyone seen where it's gone?' (2/2/1924);

and as sowing division:

Please take a look
at your internal split:
your bloated body
comes as a shock. (27/11/1920)

The appeal for black unity is a constant refrain in her poems, as Mgqwetho exploits the *imbongi*'s licence to advise and admonish as well as praise:

All black nations must merge,
unity's our only strength:
press on until you face each other,
stop your bobbing and weaving. (26/1/1924)

The guarantor of this unity is the Christian faith, particularly through the agency of Marshall Maxeke:

> Leave Reverend Maxeke alone:
>   It was God who founded that paper
>   seeing our people spent,
>   urged over the edge.
>
> When was it you were
>   elected to rule?
>   We still have our chiefs
>   established by God. (18/12/1920)

In a poem in which Mgqwetho uses the praise name by which she often addresses Maxeke, pointing to the acuity and skill of his actions, she says:

>   So says Find-at-the-Door-
>   -What-you-Shot-from-Inside.
> When we find the ford,
> we'll all kneel together,
> pleading our souls
> before God Almighty. (13/11/1920)

The irony in *Abantu Batho*'s hostility towards *Umteteli wa Bantu*, the Maxekes and Mgqwetho is heavy. Both Charlotte and Marshall Maxeke were senior and outspoken members of the ANC (with Charlotte founder of the ANC Women's Section), and the African-Christian discourse that they and their newspaper articulated was very close to that of the ANC itself. Indeed, Christianity has been thoroughly implicated in the history of the ANC, and it continues to be heard in its public rhetoric today. Christians who were all members of the founding Executive included Revd John Dube (president), Revd Walter Rubusana and Sefago Mapogo Makgatho (vice-presidents), Pixley ka Isaka Seme (treasurer), and Solomon

Plaatje (secretary). Revd E.J. Mqoboli was the first senior chaplain, and Revd H. Ncayiya, the assistant chaplain. Other Christians who rose to prominence included the Maxekes, Revd Z. Mahabane, D.D.T. Jabavu, Dr A.B. Xuma (ANC president) and R.W. Msimang (drafter of the ANC constitution).[17] Influenced by the Social Gospel movement, and particularly in the case of Dube, Jabavu and Xuma the Tuskegee model from the United States of America, these early African Christians promoted ideas of self-help and practical Christianity. Elphick points out that this group has been called by historians 'African nationalists', the 'petty bourgeoisie' or moderates, but that '[t]hey could, with equal justice, be called African Social Christians' (1997a: 357). For example, in 1925, the Revd Z. Mahabane, president of the Cape Congress and of the ANC in the mid-1920s and late-1930s, said: 'the universal acknowledgement of Christ as common Lord and King [would] break down the social, spiritual and intellectual barriers between the races' (Walshe 1997: 384). And, in 1944, Dr A.B. Xuma said that 'the liberation movement is not anti-white in seeking full scope for African progress'; rather that it was 'working for the good of all South Africans, working to promote the ideals of Christianity, human decency and democracy' (Walshe 1997: 384).

In claiming the centrality of Christianity in shaping a nationalist discourse of belonging for Africans, I do not mean to deny competing and often conflicting discourses. Prominent amongst these were those that came from the labour unions:

> The bridge-building of the Social Christians faced competition, in the early 1920s, from more radical political movements, particularly on the Witwatersrand, then a site of severe labour unrest. In the ANC . . . and in the new trade union movement, mission oriented Africans (whose enemies called them the 'good boys') were under pressure from Garveyite nationalists and Communists, both outspokenly hostile to missionaries, though not necessarily to Christianity itself. (Elphick 1997a: 359)

Labour conditions, modes of power, knowledge and social organisation, as well as economic deprivation were issues that many Christian churches – black and white – did not address directly or successfully. Mgqwetho tackles these matters head on. For her, Christianity becomes a powerful mode for addressing inequality. She describes the compulsory passbook as 'the mark of Cain' (13/12/1924); and urges political resistance on the basis of Matthew 28: 19–20:

> Go out and make disciples of every nation. Teach them in the name of the Father, the Son and the Holy Ghost, teach them to obey all those things I commanded you as law. What have we learnt from the whites? Which are the laws the Almighty commanded the whites to teach us to obey? Is it the teaching of Hertzog and the Caesars of this country? If that's the case, we just can't see the way to heaven. Oh no! (19/6/1926)

The Bible is a means of measuring the quality and commitment of leadership:

> Daniel was thrown into the lion's den and seven times into a fiery furnace and emerged unscathed. Ten times Moses was thrown against the power of Pharaoh the Lion. He came back until he triumphed. But we scatter before the Tinpot's horse!! What happens when the cannons roar? Daniel and Moses had their God indeed. And we want nothing to do with Godless leaders. (13/12/1924);

and Christianity is a unifying force:

> God bless Africa!
> Patch the network of cracks in the wall up with clay,
> so the surface appears chameleon-coloured,
> a sign to inspire our regard for each other. (2/8/1924)

While the moral basis and ballast for political resistance and criticism are provided by Mgqwetho's biblical faith, she is in no sense a 'good girl' of the missions. In response to positions such as that of Bishop Westcott, who claimed in 1900, 'We hold our Empire in the name of Christ' (quoted in Mills 1997: 341), she speaks out directly against the heresy of the white man's gospel. In the prose introduction to a poem on 28 March 1925, she says: 'Has any African minister ever preached in a white church? Why not, when there is only one God of love? Pay attention to these things!' She frequently points to the hypocrisy of the mainstream churches: 'the churches house persecution' (14/2/1925); and she links mission Christianity with colonial oppression:

> What have we learnt under the sun
> from their bibles, please tell me, my friend?
> They clapped their shackles on Africa,
> brought her low with their cannons. (2/5/1925)

This conjunction of the Bible with violent suppression, which Opland has discussed in relation to the oral *izibongo* particularly of David Yali Manisi (1999), becomes a recurrent motif in Mgqwetho's poetry:

> When the white appeared, all was normal:
> abnormality came with his bible.
>
> There was nothing casual in its preaching style:
> we saw we were completely routed.
> But when he washed the clay from our bodies
> our old men despaired, took their blankets and left.
>
> That's a grievous wound in Africa
> brought by the whiteman's bible. (19/6/1926)

In using the term 'the whiteman's bible', Mgqwetho makes a crucial manoeuvre – one that is familiar to literary studies scholars

– pointing to the fact that the 'meaning' of a text is not stable or unitary, but is a product of readers' engagement with it. The 'whiteman's bible' is not the published biblical text, but a meaning placed upon that text which is open to contestation and review. In this sense – that for many black Christians the Bible is not a text with an essential exegesis that is the sole property of learned white missionaries, but is one with which they can fruitfully engage themselves – it is ironic that many otherwise useful studies of missions in South Africa and elsewhere (De Kock's *Civilising Barbarians* [1996] is an example) never set the monologic readings of the missionaries against the biblical text itself: the implication – no doubt unintentional – is to deny agency to readers.

In this respect, Ato Quayson's critique of Christopher Miller's book *Theories of Africans* (1990) is enlightening. Quayson points out that Miller argues for a move from a discourse of totalisation to one of dialogism as constituting amongst 'the most compelling ethical models for the representation of cultures' (Miller 1990: 28; Quayson 1995: 98). While Miller has usefully theorised this endeavour, it is in fact widely evident in the self-reflexive, and self-critical, work of many postcolonial scholars, including De Kock. However, as Quayson points out, dialogising the process of representation can have the (unintended) effect of 'leaving the object observed, that is culture, relatively untouched', which allows for certain homogenising tendencies (1995: 100). We could compare the ways in which so many critics and theorists have responded to the 'conversion' of African Christians in terms of a monolithic conception of the colonisation of consciousness, whereas Christianity is far more dialogic in its experience by someone such as Mgqwetho. As the quotation from Hofmeyr on page 49 indicates, while 'common sense' would suggest that the intruding European culture of literate Christianity would overwhelm or transform the indigenous oral culture, in fact, in the initial encounter the reverse often happened. It is mistaken to assume that a stable body of Western knowledge – the Bible, the Protestant or Catholic liturgies, and so on – was simply imposed on, and ingested by, Africans. Literary studies has shown the importance of contexts of expectation and reception as well as habits of exegesis, in making sense of texts. Yet in the discussion of Christianity in an African/postcolonial context, literary and cultural scholars tend to replicate the colonial assumption that Africans were tabulae rasae: that they simply accepted the Christian message as it was understood by the missionaries with no assumptions, beliefs or understandings shaping their engagement. It is certainly true that missions often encouraged the jettisoning of all prior ('heathen') habits of belief and being; it is another thing entirely to claim that this actually happened. There is much evidence – the growth of independent churches, recent theological studies influenced by reception theory, and in this case the poetry of Mgqwetho – to the contrary.

* * *

Elphick points out that '[b]y the early nineteenth century South Africa had become one of the most intensively "occupied" fields of Christian mission in the world' (1997b: 3). However, even by the admission of the missionaries themselves, their endeavours generally met with little success. More successful than the missionaries in spreading Christianity were black converts and evangelists. Particularly among the Xhosa there were Ntsikana (to whom I shall return later in this chapter) and, with different emphasis, Nxele. In the twentieth century, African Initiated Churches (AICs) and black Christians were largely responsible for the phenomenal spread of the faith:

> Despite their subordinate position in ecclesiastical structures, Africans (and among Pentecostals, some Indians) continued to be the key agents of Christianisation in the twentieth century, most notably in the AICs, which grew from almost nothing in 1890 to embrace between a third and a half of the Africans in South Africa by the 1990s. The mission societies remained under white control, but

> by 1928 were employing almost twenty times as many blacks as whites, who increasingly served as supervisors and trainers, but not as pastors and evangelists . . . . Male migrant labourers were particularly crucial in the spread of Christianity, carrying it from missionised rural areas to the mines or city, and later from the mines or city back to the countryside . . . .
>
> The result of all this activity was a massive growth of Christian adherence among Africans in the twentieth century, a process still almost totally ignored by scholars, though it far overshadows the much slower – but more adequately studied – spread of the Christian faith in the nineteenth century. (Elphick 1997b: 7)

Particularly important for my purposes in studying the poetry of Nontsizi Mgqwetho, and my interest in religious faith as a mode of identification and belonging for many black South Africans, is the development of an indigenised Christianity. Mgqwetho's urban context, as far as can be ascertained, would have included the mine compounds and townships of Johannesburg, areas of particular focus for missionaries and black evangelists. Quayson has pointed to such sites of urban liminality as particularly formative of the kind of dialogic systems of belief and expression that Mgqwetho embodies:

> The dwellers of urban ghettos are constrained to a marginal existence at various levels, economic, political and socio-cultural. And because of the particular difficulties for upward mobility in the urban ghettos, the conditions of liminality ruthlessly persist over time. It is these conditions that generate the most nuanced understanding of the interface between oral traditions and modernity. The ideas of modernity are absorbed very rapidly, but traditional belief systems are continually activated to make meaning of ghetto existence and to forge productive alliances. (1995: 115)

In an early poem, Mgqwetho includes the lines:

> If you would return to Jehovah
> with all your heart,
> cast out from among you
> all foreign gods.
> 1 Samuel, 7.3. (15/1/1921)

The implication is that the Christian god is not foreign in the (South) African context: that Jehovah (like so many African Christians Mgqwetho favours the Old Testament form of divine address) belongs in Africa. He is given a variety of African titles and praise names – '*Simakade*' (Lord Eternal: 29/12/1923), 'Elephant eating above' (27/12/1924), 'Langalibalele's black cow' (14/8/1926), and 'Great Blanket swathing us' (4/10/1924). In addition, the biblical narrative is given local referents: 'This Christ has risen and Mary with Him./In the far Kalahari I heard the news' (10/4/1926). The source of this indigenised Christianity is the encounter of Africans with the Bible itself, rather than with the 'polluted' message of the mainstream churches:

> It's time Ethiopia joined us,
> read the scriptures and leant on them
> and stopped running off to confession. (31/1/1925)

Mgqwetho's injunctions to turn to the Word are frequent and insistent:

> Where do we stand today? What wrought the destruction and occupation of this Africa of ours? Stay calm! Examine closely that bible they used to gain access, 'God's identity'. After you suffered agony, they crushed you with it. It approached you walking backwards, not so? Made to stab at your heart? Through it offer yourself as sacrifice for your sins and you will not be disappointed . . . . (24/4/1926)

Many of the poems begin with a biblical reference, or direct readers to specific verses (almost like Bible study exercises):

> Can those twelve be found among you? If they are there, let them consult the gospel of Mark 13: 34 and Matthew 25: 14–15. Read these yourselves. The bible's here. What's not here is space in the newspaper to print what's in the bible. It's enough that I have told you where to look in the bible. (10/7/1926)

The Bible becomes evidence or proof, as in the prelude to a poem published on 22 May 1926, which is clearly influenced by the evangelical preaching tradition:

> He says he is going to prepare a place for us (John 14: 2; Hebrews 11: 16; Galatians 4: 26; Hebrews 11: 10). Who among the prophets bears witness to Jesus that he saw this place? John (Revelation 21: 2). Are we all permitted to go to that village? No! Why not? Aren't all of us who go to prayers every Sunday Christians? No! Only those who heed his instructions (Revelation 22: 14). Furthermore, those who do will see God face to face: consult Revelation 22: 2–4; Matthew 5: 8; Hebrews 12: 14; 1 Corinthians 13: 12. May he who prepared a place for us in heaven be praised: Ephesians 1: 3.

Pretorius and Jafta point to the central importance of the Bible for African Christians, in contrast, for example, to the emphasis on the role of the clergy in interpreting scripture in Protestantism and Catholicism:

> [T]he foundation of spirituality for the indigenous churches is the Bible, regarded as the Word of God, in most cases requiring, for interpretation, neither formal theological training nor commentaries. The Bible is seen as providing

> the ethical standards needed to guide worshippers in the conduct of their daily lives. The indigenous spiritual churches see themselves as closer to the Bible than the mainline churches, and closeness to the Bible is interpreted as closeness to God. Practices in the mainline churches that have no clear Biblical base, such as infant baptism, are often condemned as machinations of the devil. Prophecy, the ministry of healing, the seeing of visions, the conveyance of messages through dreams, are all believed to be based on the Bible, channels through which God speaks to the people today, as in ancient times. (1997: 224)

Gerald West, who has conducted extensive research into African readings of the Bible, suggests that – though there are divergent emphases in Bible readings in different communities – there is a common concern with its pragmatic and social implications, linked to the sense that the scriptures do not need educated exegesis, but are accessible to ordinary people (1991: 43). Interestingly, in this regard, the 'foreign gods' that Mgqwetho often enjoins African Christians to abandon seem to be not theological entities, but social problems introduced by the corrupting influences of Western society: especially money and alcohol.

When discussing the complex question of identity formation as a result of missionisation, De Kock draws on Foucault's notion of 'agonism':

> I regard the notion of agonism as crucial in understanding the apparent contradiction inherent in a missionary institution, such as Lovedale, presenting its education as a free choice, but playing a 'belligerent' cultural role in power relations, as Schreuder might describe it. Lovedale did this by promoting as knowledge a particular government of individualisation. No one was ever coerced into enrolling at Lovedale, but the pressure to be educated was such that missionary knowledge was widely desired. The concept of

> agonism also allows for the idea that while many people may have been influenced by a typical, missionary-induced 'law of the subject', they were not necessarily submissive to it in the fullest degree. My postulate is that a relationship of agonism existed, incorporating elements of freedom and coercion, in which the 'permanent provocation' of 'incitation and struggle' could never be reduced to mere domination. (1996: 36)

De Kock's purpose is to avoid the suggestion that black subjects were discursively 'trapped', and he uses the notion of 'permanent provocation' to suggest also the resistances offered. There is certainly much evidence of such agonistic relationships, particularly painfully expressed, for example, by an early Xhosa convert, Matshaya:

> By listening to the Word a struggle commenced within me, and I felt as if I had two hearts, the one loving the Word and the other hating it. After I began to attend to the Word, I became sorry for my friends, who were living in the pleasures of the world and did not see the dangers to which they were exposed. I saw that it was desirable for me to go and remain constantly at the missionary's station. (Hodgson 1997: 75)

However, while acknowledging many instances of agonism, my question is whether – as seems to be the implication of De Kock's book – it is inescapable. Especially where African Christians are not under the direct or indirect control of missions – as appears to be largely the case with Mgqwetho – they seem to live without the condition of 'permanent provocation'.[18] Unlike Matshaya who is wracked by the conflicting demands of Xhosa tradition and Christianity, for Mgqwetho the mission station is dangerous ('The Lovedale leopard slaughters our young' [28/3/1925]), and there is biblical sanction for custom and tradition: 'The truth is there in the scriptures/and also beneath our blankets' (7/3/1925). In this, her model is not white missionaries, but the Xhosa Christian Ntsikana.

Ntsikana was perceived by many as the first 'to be a Christian while remaining an African' (Mills 1997: 342–43). In a poem entitled in Opland's translation 'Something's Rotten in Africa. Listen!', Mgqwetho attributes the continent's plight to the mistaken perception that embracing Christianity entails abandoning African modes of identity:

> Ah, the grief that grips your land, Nontsizi,
> all the things that bring us grief,
> recalling our old Mgqwetho kin
> enfolded in blankets of skin.
>
> Begone with all their gods,
> their ways rip out our hearts,
> and so we don't know who we are,
> and our great men all sit mum. (29/11/1924)

The solution to this problem lies in going back to the Bible as Africans (the figure of Shaka is often evoked), not surrogate-Europeans; and Ntsikana provides the lead. Hodgson, who has written extensively on Ntsikana, explains something of his significance:

> In contrast to later converts, Ntsikana continued to live among his own people. He adopted new beliefs and practices, such as the doctrine of salvation in Christ, and new practices, such as regular meetings of non-kinship groups for worship and prayer. He maintained cultural continuity by filling elements of the Xhosa tradition with Christian content, most notably in his Great Hymn, the first in Xhosa, which drew its symbols and images from everyday life. (1997: 72)

Hodgson points out that 'the singing of Ntsikana's Great Hymn became an emotive symbol of cultural nationalism' (Hodgson 1997: 83). Indeed, in 1909, the Saint Ntsikana Memorial Association (SNMA) was formed, which

> [w]hile still firmly committed to 'progress' through Christian education . . . sought to mobilise symbols of Xhosa cultural nationalism by recovering past customs and traditions. They wore national dress at celebrations and used the Great Hymn as their anthem. Ntsikana provided an authoritative symbol to legitimate their movement: 'the blessing of God for the Xhosa nation' . . . . SNMA office holders held executive posts simultaneously in successive national bodies – the South African Native Convention (1909) and the South African Native National Congress (1912) . . . . They saw Christianity as an integrating force in developing a supra-ethnic African nationalism. Ntsikana became a saint for all Africans. (Hodgson 1997: 86–87)

While it is unknown whether Mgqwetho was herself a member of the SNMA, her constant evocations of Ntsikana's example suggest that she was fully in support of the organisation's aims:

> For whatever was written in former days was written for our instruction, that by steadfastness and by the encouragement of the scriptures we might have hope. Now listen! Didn't Ntsikana tell you to study the scriptures? And you left the whites to study them for you. I'm not mocking the white when I say that. But when it's written 'Seek and ye shall find', it doesn't mean that someone else must do the finding for you. (7/8/1926)

As the model of Ntsikana suggests, Mgqwetho does not perceive Xhosa tradition and custom as inimical to Christianity: for her the Bible and the blanket are not at odds, despite what the missionaries or white churches might say. In fact, they must be held together:

> God uses whites to oppress us:
> we spurned tradition, were beaten by lies,
> now we fight for our footing on slippery slopes. (7/6/1924)

She perceives many traditional practices as providing a structure to a society (Xhosa/African) which is falling apart both through external pressures and internal moral collapse:

> You cast aside kingship, polygyny too,
> ochre and custom in every village.
> What must we make of modern marriage?
> Wed then split: where does this come from?
>
> We sit on the fence, won't take a stand,
> the walking dead unfamiliar to God.
> It may well be true that the Xhosa like joking,
> but I have no intention of joking with you. (30/8/1924)

In a memorable metaphor, Mgqwetho summarises her position on the adoption of European ways: 'Food from another man's pot makes you fart!' (22/3/1924). One of her most powerful poems turns the resonant political slogan '*Mayibuye iAfrika*' ('Bring Africa back', 'Return Africa', or in Opland's translation, 'Oh, come back, Africa') back onto Africans themselves, who must become agents of their own liberation:

> Are you raising a cry, saying 'Come back'?
>   You'll cry yourselves hoarse: *you* must come back!
> Gone are our customs for setting up homesteads,
>   monarchy, values, nothing is left!
> You live like locusts left by the swarm,
>   you've lost all pride, your sense of a nation,
> lock, stock and barrel, everything's lost:
>   you seek balm in the bottle that blots out all pain.
>
> You say 'Come back'? *You* must come back!
>   You scratch your head in search of a scapegoat.
> Ntsikana warned you a long time ago,
>   'Money's the lightning-bird: leave it alone.'
>   (8/12/1923)

She constantly berates fellow converts for their hypocritical conduct ('We're Christians by day, but hyenas by night' [11/10/1924]), and writes extensively about the problems of alcoholism and promiscuity, and the importance of work and self-help. If Nyamende is correct about the Moravian influences evident in Mgqwetho's poetry, such teachings would certainly have contributed to her emphasis on hard work, self-reliance and a strict moral code.[19]

Mgqwetho supports black efforts to regain control of land, in particular the opportunity to purchase ground made available to the Hlubi near Rustenburg:

> We'd do well to buy land:
> I'm excited to tell you.
> Government troops clashed with Phalo's,
> we sneaked to our holes like swallows.
>
> This government from overseas
> forced thousands of people to move,
> hounded them from their shanties:
> my heart bleeds at the news.
>
> We'd do well to buy land:
> black nations must act together. (26/1/1924)

She also comments astutely on the duplicitous efforts of white missionaries and colonial officials to lure Africans into the economy of capital to their detriment. Hodgson describes this practice:

> In the late 1840s, Governor Sir Harry Smith combined his efforts to subvert the Xhosa rulers' influence with coercive measures to promote 'Christian civilisation', whether for labour recruitment, encouraging of peasant production for the market, or promoting a money economy. His politics had enthusiastic missionary support. The difficulty lay in gaining Xhosa co-operation. The Methodist, W.C. Holden,

> saw the need to create artificial wants, which would eventually take on the force of real wants and so inspire 'constant labour' in realising them. A colleague, Stephen Kay, rejoiced that 'Christianity laid the foundations of Commerce'. Missionary wives also helped introduce the market system: in 1832 the missionary's wife at Pirie taught 'the fair principles of trade' not only by persuading people to barter their corn but to sell it by the measure. At Kwelegha, Mrs James Weir purchased corn from schoolchildren, in exchange for buttons, needles, thread and handkerchiefs, and then cooked it to feed them. (Hodgson 1997: 80)

Mgqwetho's response reveals a penetrating insight into this economics of subordination:

> We're crushed by our ignorance.
> My people, we must stop selling maize:
> we'll only be forced to buy it back.
> We still use grass skirts so we starve.
> . . .
> Bright as pennies we all drink tea
> and trade our maize for sugar.
>
> Where are the customs of our land,
> transmitted to us through the ages?
> Where are the cattle and *amasi*?
> Where are the grainpits and melons?
> . . .
> When we sell our maize, we sell it cheap;
> when we buy it, the white man hikes the price. (8/3/1924)

* * *

As a Xhosa Christian woman *imbongi*, Mgqwetho speaks out boldly for her gender. One of her earliest poems is an *izibongo* on the death of her mother:

> She grazed homewards to Jerusalem,
> for her a haven of peace;
> with calloused feet this cow elephant
> smoothed life's paths for us.
>
> Torrent whose kindness
> flushed river courses,
> gush today
> in springs above Jordan. (2/12/1922)

She is constantly concerned to affirm the central role of women in her society, and to defend the right of women to speak and act. Hodgson points to the difficulties in this regard:

> The church was a significant conduit of upward mobility in class formation, with African clergy and laymen, such as John Tengo Jabavu, Elijah Makiwane, John Knox Bokwe, Pambani Mzimba, Peter Masiza, Boyce Mama, Nathaniel Mhala, and Isaac Wauchope, key figures in the educated elite. In contrast, with few exceptions, Western-educated black women only had shadowy roles in what remained a male-dominated society. (1997: 84)

Where African Christian women did have a significant, though certainly not uncontested, opportunity for voice and agency was in the prayer unions or *manyanos* (also known as mothers' unions) – 'the oldest, largest and most enduring and cohesive of all African women's organisations in South Africa' (Brandel-Syrier in Gaitskell 1997: 253). The goals of the Wesleyan Methodist Prayer Union as set out in 1913 were as follows:

> [T]o secure due recognition of the place of a Christian home in a people's life; to inculcate the moral duties of industry, honesty, truthfulness, cleanliness and kindness by example

> and precept in the home; to train younger women and girls to take their places as Christians in the national life; to encourage individual missionary effort among women not yet evangelized; and to consider any questions that affect the life of the native home and the morals of the people. (Gaitskell 1997: 256)

In *manyanos* women had – away from the direct control of male clergy – greater licence to experiment with modes of preaching, prayer and worship, especially communal and participative. *Manyanos* became renowned for the lively and fervent nature of their worship, which drew amongst other things on revivalist Christianity and a long tradition of African oral performance and dance. Indeed, two African male ministers of the American Board advised the delegates at a women's prayer union conference in Durban in 1912 'to deport themselves in a proper and tranquil manner because the officers of the Durban Corporation might get upset by the excessive noise they were making' (Gaitskell 1997: 264). As well as providing spiritual and emotional support, *manyanos* also 'undergirded popular resistance on key occasions, such as the 1913 female anti-pass demonstrations in Bloemfontein, the Herschel store boycott of 1922, the Natal beer protests of the 1920s, and perhaps even the mobilisation of the Potchefstroom women's protest of 1929 against residential permits' (Gaitskell 1997: 254).

It appears that Mgqwetho was an active supporter, as well as a member, of the prayer union called Manyano. In a poem published on 6 July 1924 she urges Manyano and a rival union, Felandawonye, to bury their differences:

> Manyano and Felandawonye!
> Why look askance at each other?
> You're both like the dews of Hermon
> Watering Zion's hills.

Manyano and Felandawonye!
Why look askance at each other?
You each command a flank in battle,
break rank only when victory's certain.

In a prose contribution later that year she offers a forthright and eloquent response to a piece from a Mr Tyelinzima Gatyeni in which he criticised women's prayer unions:

> I read in the paper *Umteteli wa Bantu* of the 16th of the month, this year, that a brother, Mr Tyelinzima Gatyeni, posed this question and ended by answering it himself: 'What has stunted the growth of Christianity?' And the brother goes on to say that he is sixty years old, and that from childhood he had known that the Word of God was preached during church services by the ministers and their evangelists alone. And that was just the way things should be. I, Nontsizi, would not wish to live that long, if with all those years I could come up with nothing logical and sensible. (6/9/1924)

In a way that foreshadows later twentieth-century feminist biblical readings, she refers ironically to the many women in biblical example who have carried their societies:

> To be brief: in other words, one should leave women of the Mothers' Unions alone, feeble creatures, to bear the heavy burden of the world's Eves, Esthers, Ruths, Deborahs, Miriams and others; the burden of the entire collapse of the world which God created; the burden of a world forgiven and redeemed through Jesus, he too, born of a woman, Mary, another woman who put her trust in prayer. With her were Elizabeth, Martha, Salome and others, all good friends of Jesus, the first to go to the grave long before daybreak, the first to know that Jesus had risen from the dead. (6/9/1924)

And she clinches the argument with some stirring rhetoric backed by biblical evidence:

> Call out 'Manyano', that's all you have to do, and applaud. Oppose this attitude. That's it, rather than criticising each other, running each other down, envying, gossiping about and betraying each other, passing on information, setting one against the other, lying. Dear oh dear! Those are the things that have stunted an enquiring Christianity and not the women of the Mothers' Unions. Never!!
>
> In the book of John, chapter 14, verses 1 and 2, Jesus Christ says this: 'Let not your hearts be troubled. Believe in God and believe also in me. In my Father's house are many places to sit. If it were not so, I would have told you.' That message is intended for you, son of Gatyeni. Trust in your ministers and their evangelists; but trust in me too, a woman of the Mothers' Union. That is what the Evangelist says. 'In my Father's house are many places to sit. If it were not so, I would have told you.' Again, that's intended for you, son of Gatyeni. There are many places for ministers to preach; there are many places for their evangelists to preach; there are many places for the women of the Mothers' Unions to preach. And there are many more places for our sons and daughters to prophesy. (6/9/1924)

Although this is a prose piece, the spirit of the *imbongi* has clearly been stirred for Mgqwetho concludes with the challenge: 'So says Nontsizi, the wing of Africa, which shelters the chicks from being carried off by other birds who prey on them' (6/9/1924).

* * *

With so little biographical information about Mgqwetho, it is difficult to account for the fact that she produced such prolific work in the period 1920 to 1926, and then published only two more poems after a two-year break. We could speculate on illness, bereavement, imprisonment, absence or harassment as reasons for the silence; or the silence may only be apparent: Mgqwetho may have published (or performed?) elsewhere. The poems that follow the silence offer no clue. They take up the idioms and concerns of those that precede them, and offer no commentary on the absence of Mgqwetho from the 'Poet's Column'. Opland claims that there is an increasing sense of despondency in her later work, which may perhaps account for the silence. He cites in particular these stanzas from her final poem:

> The year has passed, it's barely gone,
> fireworks marked its passage,
> raised voices welcomed the new,
> coming in its fashion.
>
> Now the old year's ended
> we thank you, Well of maternal love,
> for holding us all in times of peril
> throughout the year,
>
> in the world's hardships,
> the people's deprivations,
> calamities that disrupt
> our worship of God. (5/1/1929);

and comments:

> Her later poetry lacks fire, her protest is couched in vague generalisations; she yearns increasingly for the gates of heaven. At the end of the decade's first year, Mgqwetho's reaction to the afflictions of her people was to rally all blacks to unite and reclaim heroically their lost patrimony; here, in the last year of the decade, she laments their afflictions because they disrupt prayer . . . it seems the Hill of Struggle has proved too steep for Mgqwetho. (Opland 1998: 219)

If this is the case, it is difficult to know how to interpret the change: was it political disillusionment, physical exhaustion, a sense of her own impending death? Or is too large a conclusion being drawn from what may simply be a poem reflecting a particular mood, and which Mgqwetho may not have intended to be, or may not actually be, her final word? In other poems there is clear evidence of moments of disillusionment of the kind that Opland identifies:

> This hill the black man scales is steep,
> so steep it nearly daunted Christian;[20]
> his mouth frothed with a sloven's foam,
> his ears flared like a cobra.
>
> Money's an obstacle up this hill,
> envy's another obstacle:
> and so we battle to scale it.
> Can a seasoned debater dispute this? (25/4/1925);

and:

> On the plains they're stealing our mistbound cattle—
> it pains my heart to say so—
> I hope none of us is lost in the gloom
> for all our sins.
>
> The year has passed bearing news
> of nothing but persecution,
> confusion confounding
> our praise of God. (16/1/1926)

In fact, in the prose introduction to the fourth-last poem before her two-year silence, she says: 'In truth, I've given up' (14/8/1926). But in the very next poem there is evidence of a powerful faith, through which the African Christian *imbongi* declaims:

You're the Great God of heaven,
topping the white man's cannon.
You're you, the fortress of truth,
with you, shield of truth, we'll guard ourselves.
(21/8/1926)

The inadequate biographical information that we have and the ambiguity of the textual evidence make it difficult to judge conclusively on the end of her career.

* * *

On 29 May 1926, Mgqwetho published a poem with the title that Opland translates as 'Africa's Lament!! With what Pen can I Write?' With her detailed biblical knowledge, Mgqwetho would no doubt have been familiar with Psalm 45, which begins as follows:

My heart is stirred
by a noble theme
as I recite my verses for the king;
my tongue is the pen
of a skilful writer. (*The Holy Bible* 1994: 628)

In her powerful newspaper poems as a Christian Xhosa *imbongi*, Mgqwetho seems to reverse the phrasing of the psalmist: her pen is the tongue of a skilful poet who talks compellingly and assuredly to her society, and offers challenges, insights – even rebukes – to us in present circumstances.

3

'Structures of Feeling' and Constructions of History

Mazisi Kunene's *Emperor Shaka the Great*

In 1993 Mazisi Kunene was declared Poet Laureate of Africa by the United Nations Educational, Scientific, and Cultural Organization (Unesco) in a ceremony in Morocco. This declaration was greeted with both jubilation and bewilderment in South Africa. Those who approved suggested that it reflected a long-overdue honouring of a poet insufficiently recognised in his own country and continent. Others asked – mostly covertly – why Kunene should be so honoured, who felt that Africa needed a Poet Laureate, what the concept of 'Africa' implied by the title actually meant, and on what basis Unesco felt it had the jurisdiction to make such an award? And yet Kunene's being honoured as an 'African' poet by this organisation representing the 'international' community is in many ways appropriate in terms of the concerns of his work and the trajectory of his life. In addition, the combination of jubilation and covert questioning that greeted the award reflects something of the anomalous position and reception of this poet both in his own country and abroad.

In this chapter I wish to engage seriously with Mazisi Kunene through an analysis of what is arguably his best-known work, *Emperor Shaka the Great* (1979). I shall suggest the real possibilities and strengths of this poem, while acknowledging the often-contradictory 'structures of feeling' (Williams 1961) that inform and impel the poem. Kunene speaks from, and of, positions of conflicting local, national and global identification and allegiance that are powerfully evident in South African and African societies today, though his position in South African/African literary history remains curious.

Large critical claims have been made for Kunene's work by, amongst others, Albert S. Gérard, who talks of Kunene's 'considerable talent and striking originality in [his] use of traditional Zulu concepts and imagery' (1981: 217), and Kodiatu Sesay who claims that Kunene is 'certainly one of the best black writers in [South Africa] today' (1988: 61). With specific reference to *Emperor Shaka the Great*, Ken Goodwin says: 'This is, I believe, a great epic or at least one verging on greatness' (1982: 188), and Ursula A. Barnett concurs that 'it may possibly stand beside some of the world's great epics' (1983: 108). While there are frequent references in passing to Kunene in critical studies of African and South African literature, few critics can be said to have engaged with the poetry in any sustained or serious manner, or appear in many cases even to have *read* it. Those critical discussions that do exist have tended to be simply valorising (with the exception of those by John Haynes [1987], Mbongeni Z. Malaba [1988], and Ari Sitas [1994]). I wish in this chapter to give substance to the approbative claims for Kunene's work and what I perceive to be its important implications, while at the same time cutting through the mythologising of the poet and his work that obscures some of its very real difficulties.

My reasons for focusing on *Emperor Shaka the Great* are various, not least because I think it is one of Kunene's finest achievements. However, the poem is particularly fascinating in taking as its subject Shaka – one of the best-known, and most contested, historical figures in South African and African history.[1] In KwaZulu-Natal, Shaka has been appropriated by various political and commercial interest groups, and the 'story of Shaka' is in many ways the lived text of the region's past and present. As well as being taken up as a justificatory symbol or myth for much political mobilisation and conflict, the 'story of Shaka' informs almost every other aspect of life – from religious devotion in churches such as *ibandla lama-Nazaretha* (the Church of the Nazarites) and others, to debates about the location of the provincial capital and the role of traditional leaders in a modern democratic state. The image of Shaka has even recently been appropriated by the KwaZulu-Natal Tourism Board, which has promoted a recreated and Disneyfied 'Shakaland' as well as uShaka Marine World, at one stage mooted plans to build a seven-storey-high statue of Shaka at the entrance to the Durban harbour, and even considered employing a praise poet to 'lip-sync' the praises of Shaka for ships entering the Durban port!

* * *

Mazisi Kunene was born in Durban, South Africa, in 1930. His father was from the royal Swazi clan and his mother from the large Zulu Ngcobo grouping. He was educated at the University of Natal, where he completed a seminal Master of Arts (MA) study on Zulu literature (the thesis was later incorporated into the Introduction to his collection *Zulu Poems*). He left South Africa in 1959 when he won a scholarship to study at the University of London's School of Oriental and African Studies. At this stage Kunene was already politically active in the ANC, and despite his own reluctance to take up the scholarship, he was encouraged by the organisation to use the opportunity to help get the international boycott movement going (Wilkinson 1992: 140). He became the ANC's official United Nations representative (and subsequently the ANC's director of finance). Kunene travelled to Europe and the United States where he gave a number of lectures. He worked at Stanford, and was later appointed Professor of African Literature and Language at UCLA. On 1 April 1966, he was banned by a *Government Gazette Extraordinary* under the Amendment to the Suppression of Communism Act (along with a number of other black South African writers). He returned to South Africa after 30 years in exile, and in 1993 took up a Professorship in Zulu Language and Literature at the University of Natal, though he is now retired. He has published a number of poems either in Zulu or in translation, as well as several articles on Zulu philosophy and cosmology. His books include *Zulu Poems* (1970), *Emperor Shaka the Great* (1979), *Anthem of the Decades* (1981) and *The Ancestors and the Sacred Mountain* (1982).

Kunene's formative contexts as a writer and academic are very much those of Africanist debates within the ANC prior to his leaving the country, as well as the politics of exile and the agendas of African studies intellectuals in the United States. Indeed, Kunene's reputation remains high amongst many African studies scholars abroad. One of the difficulties in conducting a study of this nature from South Africa involves actually finding what has been said about him in overseas journals. Though the lack of detailed critical attention to his work may proceed in part from what David Dorsey identifies as a broader inability/reluctance in literary studies to engage in detailed poetic analysis of African poems (1988), Kunene's own historical position is clearly also significant in this regard. He was himself in exile and his books were banned for distribution (though not possession) in South Africa, and were hence not freely available inside the country. Furthermore, the tendency of literary commentaries on Kunene both in South Africa and abroad to be largely uncritical is understandable considering Kunene's own banning and the context of the broader anti-apartheid struggle that required united opposition. However, more complex engagements are not only possible now but, I would argue, necessary, if we are to evaluate fully the contribution and implications of his work; and if we are, more broadly, to engage with any success in processes of social reconstruction and national (re)definition, including contributing to global understandings of local, national and international identities.

In the Introduction to *Emperor Shaka the Great*, Kunene spells out what he perceives to be the purpose of his poem: he talks of cutting 'through the thick forest of propaganda and misrepresentation that [has] been submitted by colonial reports and historians . . . to present an honest view of the achievements of Shaka' (1979: xiii).[2] It becomes very clear in the Introduction, and in the poem itself, that Kunene's purpose is not just to exculpate the individual figure of Shaka as Zulu ruler, but to assert the importance and possibilities of the figures and institutions of African leadership more broadly. To this end, Kunene describes Shaka as 'this incredible African genius' (xxii),[3] and he frequently elides the distinction between 'African' and 'Zulu'. This semantic equation of the terms is a specific part of Kunene's project, for he is clearly influenced by Negritude and Africanist debates. However, it sets up tensions in the poem between 'ethnic', 'national' and 'international' identifications: tensions that are partly deliberate and partly inadvertent, I think, and which are matched by the ambiguities of form – and of the 'structures of feeling' – within the poem. The ethnic/national/international tensions in the poem are evident particularly to readers in present-day South Africa, as the conservative political organisation Inkatha has mobilised notions of Zulu cultural identity and history in the service of separatist political ends, specifically against the perceived Africanism or non-racialism of the ANC; while the Africanist line within the ANC, in particular Thabo Mbeki, consistently deploys a rhetoric of African unity, bordering on essentialism, to mobilise support for policy initiatives or to forestall criticism.

* * *

Before we proceed to a more detailed analysis of Kunene's poem, some discussion of the concept of the 'structure of feeling' is necessary. Raymond Williams proposes this term to describe the process of dealing with texts at a remove from one's own experience, specifically those from the past. He says: 'The most difficult thing to get hold of, in studying any past period, is this felt sense of the quality of life at a particular place and time: a sense of the ways in which the particular activities combined into a way of thinking and living' (1961: 47). This 'felt sense' is distinct from the more formally learned attitudes and perceptions that Williams refers to as 'social character' (quoting Fromm) or the 'pattern of culture' (quoting Benedict) (1961: 47). In trying to define this 'felt sense', he talks of

> a particular sense of life, a particular community of experience hardly needing expression, through which the characteristics of our way of life that an external analyst could describe are in some way passed, giving them a particular and characteristic colour. We are usually most aware of this when we notice the contrasts between generations, who never talk quite 'the same language', or when we read an account of our lives by someone from outside the community, or watch the small differences in style, of speech or behaviour, in someone who has learned our ways yet was not bred in them. Almost any formal description would be too crude to express this nevertheless quite distinct sense of a particular and native style. And if this is so, in a way of life we know intimately, it will surely be so when we ourselves are in the position of the visitor, the learner, the guest from a different generation: the position, in fact, that we are all in, when we study a past period. Though it can be turned to trivial account, the fact of such a characteristic is neither trivial nor marginal; it feels quite central.
>
> The term I would suggest to describe it is *structure of feeling*: it is as firm and definite as 'structure' suggests, yet it operates in the most delicate and least tangible parts of our activity. In one sense, this particular structure of feeling is the culture of a period: it is the particular living result of all the elements in the general organization. (Williams 1961: 48)

Williams stresses that the 'structure of feeling' does not presuppose a uniform social experience. He argues that it is not 'possessed in the same way by the many individuals in the community' (1961: 48); that (amongst other things) the coexistence of different generations within societies means that different structures of feeling may simultaneously be operative; and that a structure of feeling may (as in the South African context) itself involve a sense of division and social tension. While Williams's concern is specifically with the problems of literary history, his ideas seem to me to have important implications for writers' – such as Kunene's – negotiations of the disparate geographical, political and temporal contexts of writing and reception at home and in exile. Mongane Serote's comments about the brutality of exile for a writer suggest exactly this remove from the structure of feeling of one's home:

> I think there are very basic things a writer survives on: the minute-to-minute experiences of our people; the smells in this country; the sense that one develops when one hears conversations within South Africa influenced by local events. I was denied this. So in that regard I've always said exile is a brutal assault on writers . . . . (Brown 1992: 145)

Kunene appears to have been profoundly influenced by the Africanist line within the ANC in the late 1950s. Clearly this resonated with his own sense of the value of the social and cultural traditions within which he had been raised, and motivated his choice of subject matter for his MA thesis. In exile his concern with re-asserting indigenous cultural, social and philosophical traditions was affirmed within the pan-Africanist agendas of African politics in the 1960s, and the concerns of African studies scholars in the United States to recuperate notions of 'blackness' and 'Africanness'. Kunene in fact wrote an Introduction to the 1969 edition of Aimé Césaire's *Return to my Native Land* that indicated his endorsement of many of the tenets of Negritude.

Something of the way in which these influences swirl together into a 'structure of feeling' that permeates Kunene's project in *Emperor Shaka the Great* is suggested by his comments about indigenous literary production in apartheid South Africa. Published literature in Zulu, Xhosa and other African languages had become stultified by the system of Bantu Education and its promotion of debased versions of 'tribal' history and life. As early as 1968, Kunene had said of this writing: 'never in our entire history has literature been so childish, so trite, so aimless' (Gérard 1981: 216). In contrast, Kunene stressed that poetry should concern itself with 'long-term national and social goals' (Haynes 1987: 53), and he defined such goals as including the creation of a 'national ego' for the broader purposes of 'nation building' (Duerden and Pieterse 1982: 89). In accordance with the tenets of Negritude, he saw the rebuilding of Zulu/African society as enlarging and restoring humanity worldwide, and his definition of 'the nation' includes, at various points, Zulu people, African people and all people, a point to which I shall return later in the chapter in considering critiques of his poem.

Kunene's concern with the value of indigenous languages and traditions is reflected in the fact that *Emperor Shaka the Great*, like all his poems, was originally written in Zulu. However, it has appeared in print only in English (and in a limited Japanese edition). Kunene admits that the translation process involved some abridgement:

> The translation of the epic does not claim to correspond word for word with the original Zulu epic. I have tried to give a faithful but free translation of the original. I have also cut out a great deal of material which would seem a digression from the story, a style unacceptable in English but characteristic of deep scholarship in Zulu. (xxvii)[4]

While the decision to publish in English may be understandable in terms of market, particularly considering Kunene's position in exile and his being banned in his own country, it raises difficult questions about implied audience. In the Introduction and in the direct address of the narrator to the readership in the poem, Kunene uses first-person plural pronouns to imply a commonality between author and readership ('our national history' [xi], for example), which runs counter to his decision to abridge his epic and publish it only in English. However, it appears that Kunene is attempting to exploit the tension between a notional or implied Zulu audience and an actual international readership in presenting Shaka as a leader with specific national valencies in the African subcontinent, but worthy of symbolic stature amongst great leaders worldwide. This dual purpose of the poem is reflected in Kunene's translation strategy: 'I have eliminated the colonial terminology like "hut", "chief", "headman", etc., and, rather, based my terminology on corresponding terms in the two societies [European/English and Zulu]. I have projected the concept of power as defined by the society in question and as historically comparable with the concepts of a similar society under similar circumstances' (xxvii).[5]

Kunene's ideas about the role of poetry are clearly derived from his sense of the function of oral literature in Zulu society: he says 'it interprets, focuses and analyses the past as well as the present and then creates a perspective on the future', arguing that 'the previous generation, the present generation, and the future generation [constitute] . . . an integrated whole' (Barnett 1983: 104). Furthermore, he stresses that oral literature is meant 'not merely to entertain but primarily to teach social values and serious philosophical concepts' (Barnett 1983: 105). Copies of the English translation of *Emperor Shaka the Great* were in fact circulated to ANC guerillas in the training camps in the hope that the poem would give them a sense of renewed strength and selfhood.[6]

As a central part of his project of asserting the importance of African cultural traditions, Kunene locates himself and his poem firmly within oral literary forms and institutions. He stresses that his poem derives from oral historical sources, and claims for these an authenticity and veracity that directly oppose apartheid/Bantu Education accounts and Social-Darwinist perceptions of oral societies. In addition, in listing amongst its sources '[h]ighly trained national historians (*abalandi bezindaba zabadala*)', '[m]y uncle, A. Ngcobo' and my 'great, great grandmother', Kunene appears concerned to construct a 'history from below' (though I shall return to this point later in considering Haynes's critique of Kunene on this account). He emphasises the education that he received in indigenous literary expression and exegesis from his parents,[7] and insists that he himself has been 'chosen' as a writer in the way that an *imbongi* or praise poet would have been: that what he produces does not come from himself, but is channelled through him in some kind of prophetic/visionary way. Kunene's account of his beginning to write suggests the very real continuities he wishes to draw, and which he clearly feels very deeply, between writing and ancestral or spiritual guidance. He links the childhood stirrings of poetry within him to the sun: 'My home was on a hill or mountain overlooking the ocean, a very spectacular place, so I used to look at the sun as it came out of the ocean and it was so fantastic. I didn't know what to do about it, it just troubled me. And then it came, it just happened, there was no plan' (Wilkinson 1992: 137). And his more conscious literary production, his writing, has involved linking the symbol of literacy – the table – with that of ancestral guidance – the sun: 'When I started writing, my father brought me a small table, a folding table, so that I could go round the house. In the morning I would write on one side, facing the sun . . . then move and face the other way, always following the sun' (Wilkinson 1992: 138). In the sense of having been 'chosen' as a literate *imbongi*, Kunene sees himself as being in a direct line with the great Zulu poet of the nineteenth century, Magolwane, whom he describes as 'one of the greatest of African poets, indeed I would say one of the greatest world poets' (Goodwin 1982: 178). Kunene has himself claimed that, though he understands and accepts the benefits of the printed word, he wishes people not to read his poem but to perform it (Wilkinson 1992: 139).

Kunene describes the praise poems (*izibongo*) of the king as 'elevating the highest desirable qualities in society', and as 'project[ing] an ethical system beyond the circumstances of the individual' (xxix). Goodwin points to the changes in the tradition of praising brought about by Magolwane: 'To Magolwane [Kunene] ascribes a revolution in Zulu poetry, including the introduction of political and social analysis, penetration of character, philosophical ideas, and abundant imagery (notably of ferocious animals)' (1982: 178). Kunene's poem provides vivid accounts of praising:

> The poet celebrated the occasion with these poems,
> Speaking slowly, not throwing away his words.
> He danced leisurely, turning his body in circles.
> He moved gracefully, eager to exhibit his skill.

Even his tuft of feathers waved gently like branches in
the wind. (65–66);

and:

Yet none could surpass in skill Magolwane,
Who was the beautiful voice of the Ancestral Spirit.
He scattered words like sparks of fire.
He beat the ground with his ceremonial stick.
His voice trembled and boomed to the cliffs. (174–75)

The poem also offers some truly memorable translations of the praises of Shaka recorded by James Stuart. More fundamentally, though, *Emperor Shaka the Great* incorporates into its own textuality – into its own structure of feeling – the strategies of praising, particularly those introduced by Magolwane (the extended praise, the Shakan stanza, and so on):[8]

Angered, they marched on Khali of the emaMbatheni
clan.
They hurried to Ndonda of the Deep River;
They attacked Nyanya of the Great Dlamini clan.
They danced high, showing off their invincible weapons.
(61)

At a fundamental textual level, then, the recuperation of tradition and the validation – even valorisation – of Zuluness are woven into Kunene's poem. *Emperor Shaka the Great* also stresses the importance of *izibongo* as a means of political criticism, particularly in the dramatic intervention of the praise poet in pulling Shaka out of his torpor following the death of his mother Nandi and the destruction caused by the enforced period of mourning (344 ff.). There is probably no better text than *Emperor Shaka the Great* to suggest the extent of praising in Zulu society. As well as praising, other forms of Zulu expression are used in the poem, including prayers and songs of place:

Unto this day those who pass there sing the ancient songs.
They hear the voices of the dead as they wash their feet.
They implore the Ancestors to sing with them.
The great Zululand shall rise again! (357)

* * *

Kunene's poem is subtitled a 'Zulu epic'. There is much debate about the validity of the concept of the 'African epic', which could occupy an entire chapter, and I do not wish to engage with this question here.[9] Suffice it to say that Kunene regards *izibongo*, particularly in their expanded form following the developments of poets such as Magolwane, with other forms including historical narratives, as comprising an epic tradition that expressed 'dramatic national events' (xxv–xxvi). He refers constantly in his own poem to praise poems as being 'heroic' or 'ancestral epics', and it is clear that he sees his own epic as being in direct line with the 'epics' (*izibongo*) of Magolwane.

These epics are strongly linked with the creation of a national symbolism and founding mythology, and their function is thus very close, as several critics have noted, to Western conceptions of the epic. The definition offered by M.H. Abrams in *A Glossary of Literary Terms* could apply equally to Kunene's poem:

> In its strict use by literary critics the term epic or heroic poem is applied to a work that meets at least the following criteria: it is a long narrative poem on a great and serious subject, related in an elevated style, and centred on a heroic or quasi-divine figure on whose actions depend the fate of a tribe, a nation, or the human race. The 'traditional epics' (also called 'primary epics' or 'folk epics') were shaped by a literary artist from historical or legendary materials which had developed in the oral traditions of his people during a period of expansion or warfare. (1981: 50)

And so from the table, as opposed to the sun, and particularly the desk in California rather than the table in Zululand, come the echoes of Vergil and Homer (stressed by the diction of Kunene's translation). Textually, Kunene's poem shares many features with Western epics, including the use of set passages or 'formulae' as described by Milman Parry and Albert Lord in relation to Homer,[10] scenes of feasting and one-to-one combat, descriptions of battles, direct interventions by the gods in human affairs, prophecy, and so on. One example will suffice. After her abandonment by Shaka's father Senzangakhona, his mother Nandi is described in terms that echo Dido's predicament after discovering that Aeneas is planning to leave her:

> Hallucinations of horrendous snakes writhed around
>   her.
> They bound up her ribs; they put knots in her voice.
> She began to lose her sanity, shouting the name of
>   her lover.
> She called his name; he did not answer –
> Only the echoes came bounding from the distant
>   cliffs.
> In her madness she heard footsteps
> As if echoing from passing crowds. (8)

As well as suggesting correspondences between epic forms across societies and historical periods (which we should not simply dismiss because they sit uncomfortably with current emphases on the specificities of historical context), these echoes may be part of Kunene's project of establishing Shaka as an epic hero worthy of international reputation. They clearly fit with the emphasis in Negritude, not on rejecting the West, but on selectively reincorporating it and reinterpreting it along 'African' lines – of setting African and Western forms, and figures, beside each other as mutually influential and beneficial. This line of argument would explain the other European influences evident in Kunene's portrayal of a leader who is at once the Zulu founding figure, an African hero, and a great human leader: those of Shakespeare and of Christianity. Kunene has described similarities (though also differences) between what he refers to as the 'nationalism' of the Elizabethan court and that of Zulu society under Shaka (Duerden and Pieterse 1982: 86). Though, as Goodwin points out (1982: 181), Kunene does not attribute Shaka's downfall to any problematic aspect of his character (in fact, the epic hardly deals with Shaka's psychological or spiritual state), several of his speeches echo those of Hamlet or Macbeth.[11] Kunene also uses dramatic irony in the scene before Shaka's assassination in a way that parallels the analogous scene in *Julius Caesar*, and Princess Mkhabayi is presented as fulfilling a similar role to that of the witches in *Macbeth* (395–96). With regard to Christian influences, Senzangakhona's attempts to kill the child Shaka echo Herod's Murder of the Innocents, and the story about the generous man and the snuff has a Christ-like aspect (188).

But the 'structures of feeling' of township life in South Africa in the late 1960s and 70s, particularly as a result of developments in Black Consciousness (BC), were far removed from the epic forms of Vergil and Homer, the tragic heroes of Shakespeare, or even the heroic *izibongo* of Magolwane. Though Black Consciousness did valorise leaders such as Shaka, it did so in a rhetoric – through a structure of feeling – of the ghetto and the street. Mongane Serote's famous poem 'City Johannesburg' (1972), for example, gathers force from its ironic distance from the forms of epic praising – the salute is a search for a passbook, not a '*Bayete*' to the king – and Ingoapele Madingoane's 'black trial' (1979) is a Brechtian or Black Power epic, rather than a heroic Homeric narrative. As Mothobi Mutloatse said in his famous statement on BC attitudes to form:

> We will have to *donder* conventional literature: old-fashioned critic and reader alike. We are going to have to pee, spit and shit on literary convention before we are through, we are going to kick, push and drag literature into the form we prefer. We are going to experiment and probe and not give a damn what the critics have to say. Because we are in search of our true selves – undergoing self-discovery as a people.

> We are not going to be told how to re-live our feelings, pains and aspirations by anyone who speaks from the platform of his own rickety culture. (1980: 5)

Kunene's poem is discordant with such aggressive, 'modern' assertions, and Malaba's dismissal of *Emperor Shaka the Great* as merely a 'throwback to the slogan Black is Beautiful' (1988: 477) seems entirely to miss the point. Kunene's poem is fundamentally out of touch with the rhetoric of Black Consciousness.[12] It seems to me that the lack of response to Kunene's poem in South Africa (Sitas complains of its being 'largely unread' even in KwaZulu-Natal [1994: 151]) is less because of its banning (which did not prevent other texts from achieving popularity and influence through covert distribution), than because, from his position in exile, Kunene was removed from the structure of feeling of his South African audience. His project may have accorded with the Africanist agendas of the United States – the hagiography of the institutions of African tradition and history – but the poem seemed contradictory, anachronistic and distant because of its lofty diction, the curious timelessness and placelessness of its Western epic evocations, its promotion of 'tribal' influences and forms and its use of Zulu in the original (which were viewed with suspicion by BC activists as potentially reinforcing the social divisions of apartheid), and its remove from the cut and thrust of political mobilisation and the exigencies of evading police surveillance and interrogation.

As Williams suggests, 'ways of talking' are bound up with 'ways of feeling', and the formal ambiguities of Kunene's poem are matched by the ambiguities of his presentation of Shaka: the power and compulsion of Shaka as a great and heroic leader (and here the poet achieves great success), yet the contradictions of the poem's 'ethnic', 'national' and 'global' sympathies. In contrast to colonial and apartheid assertions of Shaka's unprecedented brutality, Kunene presents him as a wise, democratic ruler and a supreme military tactician. He emphasises particularly Shaka's intellectual abilities, including his 'scientific methods' (77), and his capabilities as a diplomat and statesman (skills he learned and refined from Dingiswayo).

While accounts of Shaka's innovative methods of warfare are well known,[13] Kunene insists that amongst Shaka's greatest achievements were both the democratisation of society, in the sense that the holding of public office was no longer tied to clan membership or family history, and the construction of a powerful national ideology: 'to be a Zulu no longer signified merely clan membership or family position, but a political grouping whose composition was inter-family and inter-national' (xx).

In accomplishing the creation of the Zulu nation, Shaka is presented as fulfilling the prophecies of his own, and his people's, destiny. From the outset there are references to 'the birthplace of our nation' (2), so that the personal destiny/greatness of Shaka and Zulu nationalism are closely linked from the start. Shaka's power is evident even in childhood:

> But Shaka of the tiger never bowed his head.
> All feared his anger.
> Even those who claimed the authority of age retreated
> from him. (29)

And almost all of the important characters foresee Shaka's greatness. His mother Nandi says:

> I knew one day my son would grow to overshadow the
> earth.
> He shall tower high above all living beings.
> The little mites that mocked us shall tremble before him.
> They shall say: 'Shaka is fearful. Shaka strikes
> But no one dares to strike him back.' (22)

His father Senzangakhona says, 'Everywhere I look I see a vision of my son Shaka' (34); and even Princess Mkhabayi in plotting his assassination says:

> In truth, Shaka's power can never be destroyed.
> It will emerge in the hearts of many generations.

They shall make their sacrifice of the black bull in his
name. (421)

Shaka's destiny to build the Zulu nation is presented in the poem especially through symbolic visions of the greatness of the 'Palm Race',[14] and this destiny is to be fulfilled because of Shaka's innovative qualities of leadership and commitment to the national ideal above all else:

He knew, too, that Shaka was like the wind
Which often lies low at dawn
But, stirred by the feet of men, leaps up to the heavens;
Yet by sunset it falls again quietly on the ground.
Such was the temperament of the great ruler of the
Zulus.
No sign or symbol or emblem was sacred to him;
Only order and the eternal visions for the Palm Race.
(365–66)

Shaka reveals himself, in Kunene's poem, to be concerned particularly with discursive constructions of nationalism, which echoes Kunene's own project in offering his poetic account of the ruler. The narrator says explicitly, 'kingdoms and states are kept intact by their poets –/It is they who embellish their tales, making the future desirable' (168). Later in the poem he[15] links such poetic performances directly with nationalism: 'The utterances of poets are like prayers to the Ancestors./The era of greatness flourishes with the epics of the nations' (246); and, more directly, 'A nation's power lies in its weapons and poems' (272). Shaka himself says, 'Zulu power no longer issues from conquest/But from a bond of an all-embracing nationhood' (199), and he affirms, 'all nations are made powerful by their rituals' (305). Indeed, many accounts of the performances of poems or songs echo the unisonality described by Benedict Anderson in the construction of imagined national communities, referred to in Chapter 2 in relation to the singing of the South African national anthem. After a performance of praise songs following a military victory, for example, the narrator affirms: 'Such were the songs that cemented the bonds of clans and nations' (177).

Notions of national identity, particularly in their overt creation and manipulation, have been the subject of criticism from a variety of positions, notably by postcolonial scholars. Yet we should acknowledge that Kunene's poem comes out of a context of social and discursive rupture: with political structures and cultural institutions and forms having been violently torn apart. So Shaka's, and Kunene's, overt nationalism and cultural assertion may be seen to be historically necessary. This is clearly Barnett's understanding when she says:

> this is not an academic or chauvinistic attempt at historical or heroic preservation, but an imaginative interpretation of African philosophy. Kunene tries to replace what Black South Africa lost under conquest: the feeling for the continuity of history, not as an object lesson for modern times, not as stimulus to nostalgia and pride, but as part of one's life. He demonstrates how we live in the past and present, and thus shape our future. (1983: 108)

Malaba's critique of Kunene for 'presenting [the reader] with a demigod, not a human being' (1988: 483), published nine years after Kunene's poem in very different historical circumstances, seems to me – despite its claimed awareness of Black Consciousness and Africanist debates – insufficiently cognisant of the pressures of the time. Instead, Malaba seems to fall back on a rather curious empiricism, stating that Kunene is simply 'wrong' in not making Shaka more brutal, etc., claims that are difficult, if not impossible, to substantiate.

In her statement quoted above, though, Barnett appears to gloss over certain real difficulties in the poem. Haynes, for example, is worried particularly that Kunene's epic is very much a 'history from above' (1987: 56), and he talks of the 'commentary-box view of battle scenes' (1987: 57). He links this criticism with the larger problem within the poem's nationalist agenda: its contradictory endorsements of Zulu and African nationalisms.

Kunene's own position both as an ANC activist/leader and a staunch supporter of the Zulu royal family is a vexed one (though Nelson Mandela reveals similarly dual allegiances in relation to Xhosa society). In the Preface Kunene says: 'I thank particularly my brother and leader, Prince Gatsha Buthelezi, who greatly inspired and encouraged me. His glorious example of leadership is a true continuation of the tradition of his ancestor, Shaka the Great himself' (xi). This is not in itself reason to criticise Kunene for ideological contradiction, for Buthelezi was himself a member of the ANC prior to forming Inkatha in 1975, and at least two other studies, clearly not supportive of Inkatha's separatist agenda, contain thanks to Buthelezi.[16] However, the poem itself makes numerous references to the greatness of the Kunene and Buthelezi clans (for example, 'Phungashe was the powerful king of the Buthelezi nation' [56], and 'There came the powerful Buthelezis of the House of Shenge' [305]), and celebrates the institutions of Zulu kingship so anxiously presided over by Inkatha (and antipathetic to Black Consciousness activists and thinkers). Kunene also assumes a basic Zulu ethic in the poem, which gives spiritual and moral weight to the notion of Zuluness. While this ethic is contrasted vividly with the stupidity, greed and arrogance displayed by the white settlers, and so becomes an effective means of political protest on Kunene's behalf, it also promotes 'tribal' understandings and divisions. And this despite the fact that Kunene wishes in the poem to 'pay tribute to all the African martyrs from Algeria to South Africa who have shared the great dream of a great Africa for all her children' (xxii), and has the narrator make statements such as 'They acclaim the swiftness in battle of the iziChwe regiment./It is truly the shield and spear of the nation' (74), which undeniably calls to mind the military wing of the ANC, *Umkhonto we Sizwe* (the Spear of the Nation). Haynes sees in Kunene's royalist sympathies a distressing trend:

> Whatever contradictions we might discern in Kunene's adherence to both the ANC and to Buthelezi, it does seem that the ideological trend in *Emperor Shaka the Great* is towards bringing the immediate struggles against apartheid under the wider sway of the Zulu ruling family, or, by extension, some form of 'top-down' populism under a charismatic 'great leader', a further 'embellishment' and 'mythification', no doubt. And this would be a 'long-term national and social goal'. To most Africans, especially those on the left, it is an ominous and familiar scenario. (1987: 61)

As Ari Sitas points out, Kunene is an 'easy target' for criticism in respect of his 'ethnic' and 'national' ambivalences:

> Of course he offers an easy target for people who are against the revival of Zulu ethnicity as a foundation stone for homeland independence, and his work could be used for such conservative ends. Despite treading such danger-zones, his work is larger than that: it is, according to him, 'a cosmic address, a prayer to life, a celebration of the great accomplishments of man'. (1994: 143)

Perhaps the ease of such judgements should give us pause, and Sitas is correct in pointing to the larger implications of the work. In suggesting that the generation and reception of Kunene's poem reflect disparate structures of feeling, I am attempting to move beyond the simple dichotomy of hagiography or rejection/impassivity of critical responses to Kunene, to serious analysis of the poem and its readings. Perhaps Kunene's poem should be set alongside other texts, and prominent figures, which reveal similar kinds of 'ethnic', 'national' and 'global' affiliations and identifications. In *Long Walk to Freedom*, Mandela describes the effect upon himself of a performance by the great Xhosa *imbongi*, S.E.K. Mqhayi: 'I felt such intense pride at that point, not as an African, but as a Xhosa: I felt like one of the chosen people' (1995: 49). Yet when

Mandela describes a performance of the praises of Shaka, his emphasis is very different: 'Suddenly there were no Xhosas or Zulus, no Indians or Africans, no rightists or leftists, no religious or political leaders; we were all nationalists and patriots bound together by a love of our common history, our culture, our country and our people' (1995: 235). Certainly modern identity politics, particularly in South Africa, involve layers and webs of competing and often conflicting allegiance and identification. Perhaps the value of a poem such as Kunene's is that critical discussion of it allows us to stage such debates openly: asking difficult questions, while allowing the symbolic power and resonance of identificatory mythologies.

We may also ask whether the poem – perhaps particularly through its elevated epic form, which suggests the possibility of symbolic resolutions – may have meanings now that would not have been open to readers in the 1970s? Are the contradictory structures of feeling capable of more productive interaction now? Are we reminded, in South Africa, of the way in which different lines of continuity – in fact, different structures of feeling – have run through our history, and continue to swirl together in the complexity of the present? Despite the overwhelming claims of BC in the 1970s, its aggressive pushing of all else to the side, many of the current leaders – at least partly because they were physically removed from society by imprisonment or exile – need to be understood in terms of the kind of heroic Africanist rhetoric that Kunene represents. Nelson Mandela and Thabo Mbeki – especially in the latter's calls for an African Renaissance – in many ways represent the continuing structure of feeling, including its ethnic/national contradictions, that Kunene's poem expresses. Mandela in particular has emphasised his connections with the rural world of custom and tradition, and we may remember that, in contrast, Black Consciousness remained a largely urban phenomenon. Perhaps *Emperor Shaka the Great*, with its accounts of life removed from the urban and industrial centre, may serve as a corrective to the urban bias in South African historiography, pointing to a sense of rural life and identification which has continued to exist, and which continues to assert its presence;

or it may remind us of the continuing resonance of diasporic Africanism in local and international relations.

Whatever the problems and contradictions of the poem, I think Sitas's reminder of Kunene's larger accomplishments and concerns, quoted earlier, remains crucial. Kunene's (African/Zulu/South African/human?) assertion of the interconnectedness of life – of the spiritual and moral obligations to others and to the future – is a rebuke and a challenge to a society that is rapidly abandoning the politics of reconstruction for individual enrichment and material acquisition. As Kunene himself put it in another poem:

> we are not the driftwood of distant oceans
> our kinsmen are a thousand centuries old
> only a few nations begat civilization
> not of gold, not of things but of people. (Sitas 1994: 143)

Perhaps this fundamental assumption – this assertion – of human interdependence is the true 'structure of feeling' of Kunene's poem.

4

Environment and Identity

Douglas Livingstone's *A Littoral Zone*

In *A Littoral Zone* (1991), his final poetry collection prior to his death, Douglas Livingstone goes some way towards answering for his own identity and location the question put to the Canadian foresters with which I began this book: 'If this is your land, where are your stories?' The collection constitutes a remarkable 'narrative' of belonging and place: of a life lived along, in terms of, and dedicated to, the coastline of Durban (in KwaZulu-Natal, South Africa) and its inhabitants – of all species.

A Littoral Zone comprises a series of poems produced over the almost three decades during which Livingstone worked as a marine bacteriologist studying the quality of sea water in the Durban region (each poem is dated by year). The volume contains, on its title page, a map of the Durban coastline and, at the end, a map of the testing stations that inspired, or are the location for, the bulk of the poems. In the cover photograph Livingstone is standing, with his testing equipment, at one of his stations. Livingstone has long been known as a poet who combines a modernist lyricism with a scientific grit, and he has been praised for his evocation of the contradictory feelings of alienation and belonging that characterise 'white African' experience.[1] Yet many readers found the overt scientifism of the volume difficult to deal with, and *A Littoral Zone* did not receive much critical attention. Recently Michael Chapman has suggested that the volume is amenable to critical recuperation in terms of the discourse of environmentalism, and that criticism beyond apartheid might return to Livingstone's work with an increasingly ecological lens (2002: xxiii).[2] However, it seems to me that notions of environment and belonging are explored in the volume in ways far more challenging and profound than that implied by 'green' awareness. In fact, I would suggest that the 'science' of the volume becomes a way of securing other claims, including that of an 'African' belonging, without necessarily privileging the 'scientific' over the poetic or symbolic.

In this chapter I argue that in *A Littoral Zone* Livingstone undertakes a remarkable project of mapping his identity and work – as poet, scientist and human being – onto the landscape in which he lived, worked and moved: that he claims belonging – in terms of myth, DNA linkages, history, biology, relationships and literature – while acknowledging estrangement – through personal loss, pollution, greed, rejection, despoliation, history, loneliness and death. The volume explores these issues in ways that are at once locally specific and broadly global: the particular place is made to resonate with wider, and profounder, implications. This does not mean that there are not also problematic aspects to the mapping of identity onto place, and towards the end of this chapter I consider some of these, including Livingstone's evocation of his relationships with black writing in South Africa.

* * *

Livingstone has been held in high regard by many critics, and received a number of prestigious poetry awards both locally and internationally, including the Cholmondley Award for Poetry in 1970, and the CNA Literary Award in 1984. Chapman said of Livingstone as early as 1981 that he was 'regarded by many people as the leading poet now writing in South Africa', and quoted in support of this verdict Richard Rive's comment that Livingstone was 'undoubtedly the best known and most highly regarded contemporary South African poet' (Chapman 1981: 9). In a review in the *Observer*, Terry

Eagleton described *Eyes Closed against the Sun* as a collection of 'clinical, observant poems, an achievement impressive in its craftsmanship' (Chapman 1981: 9). Douglas Reid Skinner suggested in 1991 that Livingstone was probably *the* major South African poet of the post-1948 period (Brown and Van Dyk 1991: 79). While Dirk Klopper, like certain other materialist critics in South Africa, has reservations about Livingstone's work, seeing in his modernist symbolism an evasion of history,[3] he points out that an examination of anthologies from Alexander Wilmot's *The Poetry of South Africa* (1887) to Guy Butler and Chris Mann's *A New Book of South African Verse in English* (1979) reveals that the canon of white South African poets generally begins with Pringle and ends with Livingstone, with critical studies suggesting that 'the most significant are Pringle, Slater, Campbell, Butler and Livingstone' (Klopper 1990: 269).

Livingstone himself frequently – and with ironic humour – rejected claims that he was a poet who had won the approval of any kind of 'literary establishment'.[4] His interview with Chapman on the receipt of the CNA Literary Award in 1984 suggests his own feeling of being somewhat 'outside' the structures of formal recognition. This sense of being 'outside' stems partly from his acute awareness of the minuscule circulation of poetry volumes, especially in South Africa, and his own employment outside of any established literary world in the apparently antithetical world of science. Perhaps more tellingly, it also comes from his own awareness that his work made difficult, often 'unpopular', assertions or connections (including those synthesising poetry and science, or criticising what he perceived as the strictures of political ideologies). Many of these challenging aspects were subordinated by critics or reviewers to praise for Livingstone's (considerable) technical skill or ironic reflection on his literary-colonial predecessors. Yet these very aspects are central to Livingstone's negotiation of place and identity, and come to the fore in the final volume, *A Littoral Zone*. I think a serious engagement with this volume suggests new ways of reading his previous work.

Chapman has produced the most extensive and perceptive critical response to Livingstone's earlier poetry (1981, 1984). He claims for Livingstone a role analogous to that of the Portuguese poet Fernando Pessoa, in that both poets, 'operating largely without the advantages of a contiguous and indigenous literary-critical tradition, have at different times attempted, almost single-handedly, to give the poetry of their respective countries voices thoroughly natural and modern' (Chapman 1984: 75). 'From the start', Chapman continues, 'Livingstone – like Pessoa – refused to see himself solely as either a "regional" or an "international" poet. *The Skull in the Mud* already signalled the emergence of a writer who, whatever his literary dependencies, pictured himself not as a disaffected "European" on a "Dionysian" continent, but as a "white African" (to use his own description)' (1984: 76). In his engagement with the local and the global, in particular the imbrication of these notions within the legacy of colonisation, Livingstone has often been read in his, partly ironic, relation to Roy Campbell. Hence – though with different emphases – Chapman comments: '[I]t is Campbell's romantically envisioned New World archetypes which inspired a parodic reaction in several of the poems from *Sjambok*, with Livingstone casting a sceptical eye on patterns of experience endemic in southern Africa and involving motifs of hunting and exploration' (1984: 74); and Klopper remarks: 'One way of describing Livingstone is to say that he is a contemporary South African modernist who combines the symbolic resonance of Campbell with the ironic sensibility of William Plomer. These points of reference describe, within the context of South African poetry, the range of poetic technique that Livingstone employs' (1990: 286). Such comparisons are enlightening, though they may sublimate the role of the scientific in Livingstone's response. Intriguingly, a comment of Campbell's suggests that this was a mode of perception with which he was familiar. In an article in *Voorslag* in 1926, he used overtly biological imagery to describe the state of South Africa at the time: 'There is no circulation, no nerve-telepathy. One aching stomach and that is all. The cells cohere in some sort of slipshod fashion but they all function in the same way. Mentally we have just arrived at the protozoic stage' (Campbell 1926: 1[2], 11–12 in Klopper 1990: 283).

* * *

In the Notes at the end of *A Littoral Zone*, Livingstone explains his title: 'The littoral zone – that mysterious border that shifts restlessly between land and sea – has, to me, always reflected that blurred and uneasy divide between humanity's physical and psychic elements' (1991: 62).[5] Many of the poems use the shoreline as a liminal zone to explore the relationship between the physical and the spiritual:

> When a cauterized synapse shrivels and dies,
> it could be some cerebral referee
> clicks on new relays to spark in that sea.
> ('Reflections at Sunkist': 14)

A 'littoral zone' is at the same time a literary zone. So the map on the title page, which gives equal space to land and sea, with the actual coastline bisecting the composition, registers the ambiguities of this physical and psychic space. Yet the volume ends with another map, which records the actual testing stations: the 'littoral zone' is also, 'literally', a scientific list of specimen collection sites. Livingstone says in the 'Notes' at the end of the volume: 'Ideally, the sequence would suggest one long poem, the record of one daylong mythical sampling run' (62). These two maps, the complex cartographic impulses that they reflect, and the poems that they enclose, represent a remarkable attempt to explore a sense of identity and belonging, which can combine microbial analysis with spiritual affinity.

What Livingstone described as his 'bread and butter job' (Thompson 1986: 6) involved monitoring the effectiveness of waste water disposal off the Durban coastline. In doing this, he developed a model of microbial testing using as indicators *Escherichia coli I*, parasite ova, staphylococci, salmonellae (including *Salmonella typhi*) and the salinity of the water (Livingstone 1989: iv) – a model that has since been adopted elsewhere. His research findings were written up in a thesis entitled 'A Microbial Study of Water Quality in the Marine Environment off Durban: 1964–1988', submitted for examination as an M.Sc. thesis in the Department of Biology at the University of Natal in Durban, but accepted as a Ph.D. The thesis contains, as its frontispiece, an aerial photograph of Durban corresponding closely with the map on the title page of *A Littoral Zone*, and includes on page 167 a map of the testing stations almost identical to the map that concludes the poetry volume. Indeed, Livingstone said that he wanted the volume and the thesis published as companion texts, and that the 'hard core version' of the poems is the thesis.[6] Both represent the culmination of a life, and a life's work.

Livingstone's engagement with the sea combines biological acuity and spiritual devotion with a profound sense of self-irony (Don Quixote is a recurrent motif):

> There's work ahead: futile,
> scientifically delivered blows at sullage,
> against the republics of ignorance and apathy,
> with bust lance, flawed shield,
> lamed steed of action; downhill
> past Country Club to Blue Lagoon
> brown with silt hell-bent for the surf.
> Here is my daily bread's commencement.
> ('Starting Out': 10)

The crucial manoeuvre – which is evident in Livingstone's previous work but becomes explicit and pervasive here – is to refigure the place of humans in the broader context of biologically conceived, but nevertheless spiritual, life. Central to this is the Gaia principle, according to which the Earth is conceived of as a living cell and about which Livingstone comments: 'I look on the earth as a living cell, much tougher – as a whole entity – than humanity. And the cell *could* unconsciously muster all its resources – from viruses to volcanoes – and turn on and rend the life-form that subjects it to so much stress and abuse' (Thompson 1986: 3–4). In this explicitly anti-anthropocentric vision, proper human conduct is defined in terms of biological symbiosis (a word that recurs in the poems): the ability of life forms to coexist to mutual benefit. Indeed, a sense of belonging, or of alienation, is often registered at the level of species. One of the most disturbing poems, 'Carnivores at Station 22' (55), describes the speaker's futile attempts to return a beached dolphin to the water. The title deliberately displaces human behaviour into the biological context: people become 'carnivores'; the fishermen are 'birds of prey' who 'stab sea and sky with bamboo beaks' (their rods). Their response to the speaker's pleas for help is to 'look away', for they perceive the dolphin simply as bait or food. Thus they are damned in the poem as a species ('I offered up a curse on *Homo sap*'), not as individuals with moral choices. The speaker's compassion for the dolphin is not offered in terms of its perceived intelligence, humanity or beauty, but in the biological contract between species:

> The paradox has always haunted me:
> these are the only carnivores on earth
> that have never attacked man, yet
> out of their element they gain new worth. (55)

It is humans who are the ugly species in this encounter:

> As I left, the fishermen stirred: stashing
> rods, moving in that ugly minuet
> of deliberate premeditation,
> one drawing a long and rusted bayonet. (55)

Similarly, in the poem 'Cells at Station 11' (35), the question of ethical conduct is engaged at the level of the cell. While he is collecting his water sample, the speaker spots 'a blackened corpse' out to sea, which raises the question of moral action for him. Yet the answer comes not from philosophical meditation but through the lens of a microscope, as he realises that his water sample may contain a cell from 'that out there', and he perceives the death in terms of cellular fratricide:

> Woe will betide, betimes, the man
> who kills his brother: burns shared cells
> – those bound lovers under the sun –
> lolling there in an unchecked sea. (35)

In his paper '"Africa Within Us" . . . .', Livingstone elaborated on this notion:

> A living body is of course subject to certain immutable laws. A body divided against itself, as someone I'm sure said, dies – as in various types of cancer for instance, where some cells, not content with their orderly dissimilarities yet underlying unity of purpose with the blokes over the road, differ yet again from their associates, and in trying to impose their ways on the others, destroy the whole world they occupy. Dying too in the process, of course: the inexorable final goal of which they are no doubt mindlessly aware while the heady process of Antigone-like resurrection ensues. (1976: 143)

The despair implicit in this vision is counterbalanced by the hope that resides in the resilience of life forms. Thus, in 'Scourings at Station 19' (47), there is a guarded optimism in the incongruous sight of a bantam cock on a pile of debris following the devastating floods of 1987:

> On one high peak, (a pain for the SPCA
> if ever there was one!) a roughed up bantam stands
> still handsome if glazed, his feathers skew; orange,
>   brown,

scarlet and black dusty with sand and wrung out brine
– no steepled vane yawing above ordered pews here.
(47)

The humour reflects admiration for the spirit of the bird,[7] which calls out its territorial challenge amid chaos and destruction, asserting its life – or the resilience of Life in general – despite all odds. The concluding lines are qualified by the word 'tempting', for the informed scientist, and the insightful poet, are well aware of the odds stacked against the rooster and all it represents: 'Tempting to dub the din thanksgiving; or more: life/triumphs even on no longer trusted planets'.

In response to such perceptions in Livingstone's earlier poetry, Klopper is critical of what he sees as the inappropriate transposition of the biological onto the human-moral: 'A crude view of biological survival appears to have been elevated to a transcendental absolute and applied equally to animal and human societies' (1990: 289). Indeed, Klopper perceives the biological or scientific as simply constituting a new mode of transcending the difficulties of history:

> But then Livingstone has chosen to disavow what he scathingly terms 'Polit-Lit' (1976: 142) and has adopted, instead, a form of individualistic response which is directed at the discovery of the universal (rather than historically specific) truths. Accordingly he continues the Romantic tradition that I have been examining in this article. In terms of this tradition the artist is deemed a highly developed and attuned individual who is in a position of privileged insight and uncommon talent *vis-à-vis* his society.
>
> What sets Livingstone's transcendentalism apart from other transcendentalisms that I have been discussing is his privileging of science (rather than God or spirit or self) as the ultimate source of truth. (Klopper 1990: 289)

In an interview, Livingstone responded to a similar criticism as follows:

> I am not at all convinced that humanity alone has the complete title-deeds to the earth, or to the minds and hearts and souls of all other humans – i.e. that Collective Man is the overlord to all men and everything else. And the finest piece of 'useful' art I ever saw was a perfect spider's web, dew-drenched at dawn. (Thompson 1986: 7)

I think Klopper himself is open to the charge of elevating 'history' above 'biology', ironically in view of the obvious connection between the biological and the economic in the means of production. While I do not necessarily myself endorse Livingstone's position, it does seem to me to take full account of the materiality and morality of life, while allowing also spiritual affinities:

> Somewhere in between those two, between labourer and super-scientist is the problem of uncontrolled population increases, industrial sinfulness towards the earth in disposing or dumping of our waste products; then there's food – hungry bellies – and clean water – general health – and well-being – not just for the privileged few going for their corneal or cardiac transplants. (Chapman 1985: 96)

A poetic vision that can hold in balance the arterial reticulation of effluent disposal in the Durban region with the gesture of poetic affinity, while it may reveal other problems, seems to me somewhat resilient to the charge of historical dereliction.

In *A Littoral Zone*, the scientific and the poetic interplay in ways which – while they are gestured at in Livingstone's previous work – point to new modes of perception, analysis and critical-creative expression: which can articulate the notion of knowing and living the particular place with the broader understanding of how one knows or lives place at all. As a term such as 'industrial sinfulness' indicates, this involves new conjunctions of the spiritual and analytic in ways which suggest that the co-publication of poetry volume and biological thesis may not be as bizarre as we may initially think:

> I have always had quite a strong impulse to heal my fellow man, medically, and, sort of quasi-medically to heal the earth, this wonderful planet we live on – this space-ship we are all condemned to serve our time on. I work in marine bacteriology against the pollution of water; and I have all kinds of psychic and mystic connections with water, as I do with the sun. I don't think anything – not one thing I've mentioned here is incompatible with poetry. I think they are all interconnected with all aspects of literature and aspects of science. (Chapman 1985: 95–96)

In a paper entitled 'Science and Truth' – which he published as D.J. Livingstone and described to me as something he felt was one of his best pieces of writing[8] – he expands upon the new, integrative possibilities of knowledge:

> In our own era, the multi-level ontologists epitomised by Whiteman, with formidable if tangential support from such daring intellectuals as J.E. Lovelock, Lewis Thomas and Nicholas Humphrey, afford us the glimmerings of the whole as one. 'Journeys into space did more than present the earth in a new perspective . . . From this has arisen the hypothesis, the model, in which the Earth's living matter, air, oceans and land surface form a complex system which can be seen as a single organism . . . and has ranged through the territories of many scientific disciplines, indeed from astronomy to zoology' (Lovelock 1979). 'Viewed from the distance of the moon, the astonishing thing about the earth, catching the breath, is that it is alive . . . it has the organised, self-contained look of a live creature . . . It takes a membrane to make sense out of order in biology . . . You have to be able to catch energy and hold it . . . A cell does this . . .' (Thomas 1983). 'Beautiful "structures" in nature or art are those which facilitate the task of classification by presenting evidence of the "taxonomic" relations between things . . .' (Humphrey

> 1984). The corpus appears to be not so much the life *on*, but the life *of* the Earth; and the singularities of such a vision must consequently 'provide the basis for a truly unified philosophy of science and nature', to borrow John Poynton's (1985) felicitious phrase. (Livingstone 1986: 105)

Hence in 'Road Back' (60–61), the poem that concludes *A Littoral Zone* and the mythical day's sampling run, a vision is offered which conjoins the astronomical-planetary, the biological-cellular, and the literary-romantic (again in the figure of Quixote):

> A tendency in all that's living is to excrete
> its entropy. The planet counterattacks.
> Its choice is plain: kill or be killed.
> Ours too: symbiosis or death
> at the hands of a bright blue cell
> – the only living thing in known space.
> Perhaps you do not need your knights, Gaia:
> in the end you have to win. (61)

The very notions of scientific and poetic 'truth' begin to coalesce, with the poem and the scientific constituting equally 'raids on the inarticulate':

> It is possible we have to reconcile our pursuit of scientific truth – verifying every step of the way, imagining it, longing for it, even dreaming of it, spurring ourselves on with the current theory or available ratiocinative device, alert always for the dissolution of rigidities whose compartments re-form into new realities which will dissolve in their turn – with never actually attaining it. Einstein's observation: 'The most beautiful emotion we can experience is the mystical. It is the source of all true art and science', affords not only comfort but enjoyment while the day to day proper business of science ensues, i.e. seeking after truth, however evasive the truth happens to be. (Livingstone 1986: 106)

I think Narismulu (1986) is correct in this respect that Livingstone's professional involvement with science explains why his poems appear to represent models, that is, approximations that are valid for a certain range of experience – beyond which they have to be either revised or replaced. The longing to

> . . . restart
> a cycle of maybe something more pastoral
> commencing with beetles, then maggots, then ants

that concludes 'Gentling a Wildcat' (1970: 19), is revised in the 1981 poem 'Bad Run at King's Rest' in *A Littoral Zone*, in which the injured turtle – unlike the wildcat, it has been injured and then tortured by humans – is killed to prevent its further suffering:

> I moved – lifelong stand-in for thought –
> avoiding the still dangerous beak,
> asking pardon, cut the leathery throat.
>
> Rinse off queasily. Circle wide,
> back, past that inert, spread-eagled mound.
> Call dumbly on incoming tides. (37)

Chapman comments that '[u]ncertainty is this poet's authentic poetic and philosophical attitude', though it is the uncertainty of the working hypothesis, rather than that of liberal, or postmodern, helplessness: a desire for 'synthesis amid indeterminacy' (1984: 96, 102).

The term 'pardon' in the poem quoted above evokes the religious that is integral to the poetic-scientific mode. Livingstone has said: 'No one can be a serious scientist, even in the natural sciences, with an interest in physics and sub-atomic particles, and proclaim: there is no God' (Fazzini 1991: 139–40); and that he has 'an inkling that all life is interconnected and ultimately holy; that we are, temporarily, in a temple of life' (Fazzini 1991: 142). Hence the poem

'An Evolutionary Nod to God: Station 4'. One of the strengths of *A Littoral Zone* is the way in which a rigorous biological understanding of life echoes with spiritual wonder: in the section quoted earlier from 'Starting Out', his work is his 'daily bread's commencement' (10); the coelacanth in 'Address to a Patrician at Station 8' is 'Ancient funny-bone of God' (24); and the encounter with a duiker doe in 'A Visitor at Station 21' (53–54) is 'an impending holy event'. Finally, in what I think comes as close to a credo as anything Livingstone has written, he concludes the opening sonnet, 'A Darwinian Preface' (7), as follows:

> . . . that old vortex
> steeled by the usual mundane heroisms.
> Your heart wins armour from confronting life,
> yet stays unlatched, anticipating love.
> Each dawn claims thanks and welcome, gets blessed.
> Perhaps the sea indeed did suckle you
> through all its prisms, its diurnal rage.
> There is no help for it. Best buckle to. (7)

* * *

Es'kia Mphahlele has been critical of what he perceives to be the aloofness, arrogance and ignorance of many white South Africans who refuse engagement with the place and its people:

> The white man, for his part, refused, as he still does, to admit that his own ways had changed, and that the presence of the African had a lot to do with it. He still attempts to shut the black man out of his private and public life, out of his dreams, out of those recesses of the personality where the myths of the tribe reside. He claims to be African while he pretends to be above the indigenous majority culture, while he glories in the imagined superiority of Western civilisation and behaves as an extension of it. (1987: 52)

From his first publication *The Skull in the Mud*, in 1960, Livingstone has refused that remove, and instead explored the paradoxes of his position as a white African. In the notes for his play *A Rhino for the Boardroom* he talks of his deep sense of connectedness with place:

> My involvement with this continent as a white African is to me a profound and passionate and (I hope) compassionate one. If I could I would heal the very earth on which we stand, the waters I sail on, swim in, work with, look over, drink from; and of course, myself, my fellow humans and the fauna and flora. The only scalpels and medicaments I have are a limited scientific training, a little insight and a small writing talent. (1977: 21)

In its literary-cartographic impulse, *A Littoral Zone* extends this concern. The exploration of white Africanness is bolstered by the commitment of a life dedicated to the health of the sea, but also by the scientist's awareness that the microns of differing skin pigmentation to which colonial and apartheid ideologies have attributed such significance are genetically insignificant in comparison with the biological commonalities.[9] What is meant by being African is open to new possibilities, and – as I have suggested – Livingstone explores kinship at the level of DNA linkages, as well as shared moral responsibility for each other and the planet, though especially what he calls this 'heart-shaped continent' (Chapman 1985: 93–94).

As well as through scientific or biological engagement, Livingstone claims identity and belonging in an almost De Certeauian sense through habits of movement and knowing. The official maps that enfold the poems are offset by various accounts of unofficial moving through and in space. The prefatory sonnet already mentioned, 'A Darwinian Preface', is followed by the opening poem, 'Starting Out' (8–10), which offers a detailed account of driving to begin the sampling run:

The Cortina is already loaded with boxes
of wide-mouthed glass sampling bottles,
aluminium racks of plastic ones
and a sampling stick that clacks its jaws.
To horse! The whole wagon will sound
like a milk truck if I do not leave slowly,
saving the door slam for the street.
The suburb approaches, still fast asleep. (9)

And the concluding poem, 'Road Back' (60–61), offers a more disturbing view of the return, in which place becomes almost surreally menacing:

Driving's a lethal skill: its ease
fatally invites domestic reprises
– the whole substructure steered and toed
by the doomed and hurtling microcosm within.
Tyres scream softly as they thud
and thin; a spring, bolt or pin
crystallizing as it slams its wishboned way
along the waiting roads unbandaging in advance. (60)

Seamus Heaney's phrase 'lost, unhappy and at home' springs to mind here (1972: 48). Throughout *A Littoral Zone* there are accounts – by turns welcoming and threatening – of physical intimacy with land- or seascape: 'rubber soles . . . for bounding over barnacles' (8); 'Nine steps climb to a pair of spinster geraniums/pot-shod' (19); a one-legged man 'hops robustly from the surf' (22); 'About nine months ago I slipped/right here, slicing my left heel open' (25); 'stumbling, weighed with the long sampling stick' (36); 'Without you, the/sand underfoot reels disrupted' (40); 'dumb slithers, stumbles, lacerated skin/a rock-hobbled ankle' (44); 'plodding softly in sand-shod stealth' (48); 'small hooves/tread delicately, pause for each wave-/break' (53–54). Livingstone evokes familiar movement as a claim for belonging in the way that the nineteenth-century

/Xam Bushman narrator //Kabbo claimed his land – amongst other ways – in terms of his intimacy of understanding and knowledge (see Chapter 1). Particular locales are vividly imaged, including the old whaling station on the south side of the Durban harbour in 'Beach Terminal' (36):

> The old whaling station is ship-wrecked;
> corrugated roofs, zinc walls flaking;
> most of the cataracted panes smashed;
> the sea clean now, the sand still tarry. (36)

Then there is the rubbish strewn around Blue Lagoon following the Christmas revelry in 'The Christmas Chefs of Station 1A' (12):

> The mess on the sand incredible:
> scraps, vomit and cartons abound.
> Most redolent of Decembers!
> Here, one has out-sphinctered a newt.
> That bent fish looks once-edible
> but, judging from the fat spilled around,
> meat was grilled on the embers;
> crushed beercans and ashes lie mute. (12)

There is also a community evoked in *A Littoral Zone*: figures of closeness; flashes of intimacy with strangers; lovers (real or imagined?); closely observed passers-by; mythological figures with the charge of the real; and literary forebears. A 'littoral zone' is a humanised, if not always humanising, landscape – though the effects of human company or habitation are often destructive, to the speaker as well as to other species or habitats. As Chapman has suggested:

> Sea, sand and rock are the deep constants against which the poet places the sometimes strident, more often vulnerable participants in the everyday business of civil living: beach-goers littering the sand after a picnic, the clearing of a

> polluted bay, the grandeur and comedy of small people in a large universe where God, or the gods, or the stars may, or may not, look down on the creatures of creation. (1996: 343)

Amongst the most compelling in the collection are the love poems in which a longing for, or achievement of, closeness and touch is balanced against the awareness of loss and loneliness. In 'An African Loving, Station 3' (15), the erotic charge of the first stanza:

> There was your first sunblinded glance.
> Sand tracked the long hot morning
> which turned to a merry barefoot dance
> – damp kisses without warning. (15),

gives way to abandonment:

> Then you were gone. My dry beached fright
> knew no life ahead, alone.
> Returning to claim me in the night,
> your womb had turned to stone. (15)

And in 'Subjectivities at Station 15' (40), it is again parting and dissolution that are portrayed:

>   Without you, my
> balancing act's deconstructed.
> Clouds gorged with menace lower.
>   My blood feels thinner
> the torn homeless sea corrupting. (40)

Some of the chance encounters mirror the kind of community of urban dwellers that Livingstone has evoked so effectively in his previous work. They are Eliotian figures of alienation and longing, but with the living particularity of place:

> A last blink from suburbia: the hunched crone
> Shaking out her khelims. She once said
> she'd had an affair with Vincent Swart . . . (10),

and:

> She still comes to South Beach
> to sew. Our touchstone missing,
> we do not speak. (22),

or:

> Then a dolphin-dusky prostitute teeters
> from an expensive house . . .
> . . .
> I allow her extra time to cross
> at the light and relish my reward in her smile. (9)

Other members of the community are vividly retained in the memory long after one closes the volume, including the loquacious proprietor of the café on the Isipingo River, Rivermouth Singh:

> A whitewashed pane cheers the road to sand-plugged
> Isipingo's river mouth: 'Rivermouth
> Singh is a fart.' ('*Au contraire, mon ami,*
> I'm all heart.' His right hand palms it. His French
> – broad P C Wren – 'is coming from the past;
> Pondicherry; unlettered parents, dead.') (59)

There is also the retired white Colonel with a fondness for young Indian girls (the poem predates the abolition of the Immorality Act):

> The Colonel (Retired), guilt-wracked
> (what else, here?) and pallid, thrashes away
> from three lovely nubile Asian girls
> – all giggles, stretched lycra, wet slenderness.

He teaches crawl and breaststroke, risking much.
His panting hairless bulk gains turf, and heaves
towards towel and beta-blocker pack. (59)

As 'real' in this landscape are the mythological Darryl Hook, drowned for the love of his mermaid off Cracker Reef (31–34), or the poets Roy Campbell and Fernando Pessoa whose presence still haunts the speaker's memories of the old harbour (26).

Even in the satire, there is deep compassion for the place and its people. In an interview with Chapman, Livingstone says of this: 'It's like a marriage – isn't it – full of anticipated surprises: periods of troubled love, of hate, understandings, and misunderstandings. There's a deep, slow river of love in me for the land, its denizens, its waters, its skies' (Chapman 1985: 93–94). This compassion includes a profound (and scientifically anchored) rejection of racism: 'I *know* such intolerances as antisemitism, racism, etc. to be inimical, incompatible with the spirit of being truly human, and, in the long term, biologically doomed. Tribalism has, of course, quite a road to run, especially in the Northern Hemisphere!' (Chapman 1985: 93).

Yet – perhaps in terms of a radical dislike for the conformity of the group[10] – he has tended to caricature revolutionary social action, lapsing instead into a kind of biological determinism or (racial/ cultural/continental?) essentialism:

> Now, this may make me even more unpopular – few speak the truth about Africa – I think we could do worse than forget our 'first world' pretensions for a century or so, and accept we are, all of us here 'third world'! In case anyone thinks that's derogatory, let me add at once: I prefer the third world – it's more cooperative, less competitive, more alive yet less frenetic, less materialistic, closer to the earth and its blessings and cursings; in a strange way more spiritual. There is a tough side to this: there is a cliché – 'Africa is dying'. It is, of course: about 10 to 15 ha (about 30 acres) of rainforest is being destroyed every 60 seconds, with all *that* implies; while first

> world technology saves and guides more hungry bellies through the thorns of natural selection merely to dump them on the expanding deserts of a bleak future . . . . Something else, equally uncomfortable, we all have to face – a biological fact of life on this heart-shaped continent: in Africa the strong man rules. Not the good, the bright, the virtuous, the democratic or the just, but the strong. I'm sorry about this because I'm also a bit of an idealist. I foresee no change – apart from possible external subjugations, re-colonisations – for some dozens of years. The brief toyings with variations of democracy will, I believe, be looked back upon as historical curiosities. Or as well-meant aberrations. If man is merely another biological life-form, this principle – the strong ruling – will eventually obtain, even in the West. It already mainly obtains in the East. If there is more to man – and I fervently hope there is – than the biological reductionists would have it, then happier scenarios *could* happen. Otherwise, it's Dictators ahead, and in all directions. One can only hope grimly for benevolent ones. (Chapman 1985: 93–94)

While Livingstone claims here his own hope that the biological model is not all-explanatory of human behaviour, there is little in *A Littoral Zone* which presents action for political change in South Africa – rather than the 'ordinary' business of living – in positive terms. Perhaps in this sense, Klopper's critique – referred to earlier – is valid: that Livingstone's scientific determinism may problematise the question of human agency.

* * *

A further difficult aspect of Livingstone's narrative of belonging in *A Littoral Zone*, perhaps connected to his pessimistic view of revolutionary action, is his evocation of his relation with black writing. For instance, in 'Beachfront Hotel at Station 5' (19–20), the rather overwrought description of the decaying establishment:

> The sunk huddle of a patch of bedding shirks
> on sagging outcopulated bedsprings upheld
> wearily afloat on the upright wood and weld.
> Disapproving drapes rustle worn calico skirts
>   at cycloped pairs of electrics. (19),

is followed by the speaker's discovery that the drawers are lined with old copies of *Drum* magazine:

> Within the wardrobe, a rich yellowing treasure
> spreads of leaves from *Drum*: crouched boxers,
>   bronze beauty queens;
> Todd Matshikiza, Can Themba, news of shebeens
> – the Runyonesque wit taking the land's bleak measure
>   even to the lost shores of gaols.
>
> In shallow warped flimsy ill-fitting drawers slide lined
> sheets of Nat Nakasa and Bloke Modisane;
> of Casey Motsisi and Arthur Maimane;
> pages of Lewis Nkosi; while a piece signed
>   Ezekiel Mphahlele sticks. (19–20)

The poem is dated 1964, and indicates perhaps Livingstone's greater sensitivity to, and awareness of, black writing than has hitherto been acknowledged. (Many white readers only became familiar with *Drum* magazine through the 1990 publication of Michael Chapman's anthology *The Drum Decade*.) Yet besides remarking on the finding of the *Drum* pages, the poem does nothing with them. They seem simply to happen into the poem as they (presumably) happened into Livingstone's own experience; the question of writing place, in relation to what others of one's society are writing, is ignored. In another poem, Livingstone does attempt to explore this question, but in my opinion with even less success. 'The Waste Land at Station 14' (38–39) presents a satirical portrait of a rabble-rousing black poet, whose real muse directs him to write secret lyrics to the African moon:

> Shozi Bhengu, the literary star,
> could pack a hall or church with raucous crowds
> applauding his poems. He'd yell for shrouds
> to wrap the sell-outs. He was called the Czar.
> 'Death,' he would roar, 'to the northern invaders,
> honkies are but sacrificial goats.'
> . . .
> Still, within his skull, the swivelling prism
> of hatred, love, the racist catechism
> – well learnt – would not quite jell. 'When I am dead,'
> he told his wife, 'that file under the bed
> (choose a moment which looks most opportune)
> holds my lyrics to the African moon.' (38)

It is not clear how we are to take this, particularly as it is followed by the speaker's (intentionally?) bathetic interjection:

> What the hell!
> I might just as well
> have writ the same
> if Shozi Bhengu were my name. (38)

My own reading of this is that Livingstone's wariness of political rhetoric and the conformity of the group lead him into a parodic, dismissive and inaccurate portrayal of important aspects of black writing. This is both ironic and unfortunate, for Livingstone's own critical comments about black writing from South Africa suggest a degree of openness to different aesthetic possibilities. His discussion of the process of translating Shona poems indicates the seriousness with which he approaches their aesthetic form (Fazzini 1991: 143–44), and in *A Littoral Zone* the poem 'Address to a Patrician at Station 8' (24) uses the form of the praise poem with some success. Though Klopper is critical of what he regards to be Livingstone's 'formalism, his exclusive consideration of European poetic techniques and his notion of the autonomy of the poet as craftsman' (1990: 290), I think a more nuanced reading is required. In talking of 'international yardsticks', for example, Livingstone said: 'Poetry in English, in Africa, must be judged fairly, I think, by internationally accepted yardsticks. *If the poetry is powerful enough and causes those yardsticks to change – so much the better!*' (Livingstone 1982: 157, emphasis added). He talked of the need to 'expand our literary base, hopefully into larger African directions, not American ones' (Chapman 1985: 98), and he praised the Soweto poets for their emphases on piety, filial devotion and community (Livingstone 1982: 160). This is not to deny problematic aspects of Livingstone's critical writing, or to efface the difficulties of the evocations of black writing in the poems discussed above. It is simply to refute the simple, knee-jerk response that Livingstone endorsed European standards. His serious, though not solemn, attempts to find an appropriate form and voice demand a more complex response.

More successful than his attempts to explore belonging in terms of black writing is his poem, 'Eland about Station 17' (44–45), in which he considers Bushman rock painting as an expression of identity which resonates with his own, but which also speaks of colonial atrocity and genocide. When the speaker happens upon a cave on the Bluff, now 'covered by landfill to buttress the housing and roads above' (62), he discovers that its walls are covered with paintings:

> The stone sides are crammed: blazed
> with swarms of symbiotic man about
> the business of getting on with the earth
> – my fathers, such candour! – and it with him,
> some mantid-cowled; with a dolphin displayed
> beside, up there, one wondrous elephant. (44)

Unlike what seems to me the caricature of Shozi Bhengu, these artists are understood in the complexity of their mythological representation:

> the running crouched abduction followed by
> the murder of Kogaz, son of a god
> named Xagen who then magicked every one
> of those first kidnappers into baboons.
>
> Thin shamans dance their spells, or meditate
> themselves through the souls of eland to purge
> an evil from the tribe . . . (44)

This awareness translates not into the rather mawkish apology to Bhengu for the apartheid beach sign ('For you, Shozi, this final line:/ my apologies for that sign' [39]), but a real recognition of the brutal history that is inextricably bound up with a white African identity:

> There is much I cannot forgive my race.
> Parched cryptic ones, you have been hunted and herded
> to the westward wastes – all that's left of you:
> now learning metallic intricacies
> of automatic weaponry. The least
> I can do is keep this cave hid for you,
> mounting no sign and exacting no due,
> having called, stroked and dreamed into eland. (45)

The act of concealment and the fact of the poem constitute small acts of resistance and reparation.

* * *

I think Chapman is correct in asserting that 'Livingstone's South Africanness may yet be identified in the capacity of his poetry to provoke strong debates about the responsibility of the poet in a society of scarce resources and narrow tolerances, in both economic and literary life' (1996: 343–44). *A Littoral Zone* is a text of problems and possibilities, which challenges us on the central questions of South African, African and human/non-human life: of how we live on, in and with a place and its people and its life; how we can claim to belong, and what it means to do so? As Livingstone himself pointed out in an interview – and in this volume – this is a question that demands attention:

> With the miracle of tolerance our weaknesses could be transmuted into a mutually enriching strength. South Africa is the world's laboratory: it represents the globe's nations and preoccupations in the microcosm. If it fails – and the divergences are enormous – there is no future for humanity at large except the ugly spread of racial and religious wars, the final triumph of evil in pursuit of the devils of materialism, power and mindless destructivity.
>
> In which case we deserve to go, allowing the planet to recover from our hubris, gather its resources to prepare for a more symbiotic and less quarrelsome species. (Fazzini 1991: 145)

5

Narrative, Memory and Mapping

Ronnie Govender's *'At the Edge' and Other Cato Manor Stories*

> [There is] an elaborate frame through which our adult eyes survey the landscape . . . Its scenery is built up as much from the strata of memory as from layers of rock.
>
> *Simon Schama (Darian-Smith et al. 1996: 10)*

The African protagonist of one of Ronnie Govender's short stories walks along Cato Manor Road:

> He walked past the Jew's shop which was where the white area started at the top of Cato Manor Road, the long road on the border which dissected the Indian area of Cato Manor from the area of the Berea. Onwards to Concord Road which was a short, neat road flanked by staid brick-and-tile houses which could have been transplanted from some lower middle-class English suburb. Their inhabitants in shorts, floppy hats and sweaty red faces battled constantly to severely prune lush sub-tropica in a bid to transform it into lifeless gardens of well-ordered rows of hydrangea and meticulously manicured bougainvillea hedges. Dumi would contrast this soulless uniformity with the way nature celebrated the gift of life with such marvellous abandon on the banks of the Umgeni River, as it wound its way through the Valley of a

> Thousand Hills where he grew up as a child. (1996: 108–09)[1]

The year is 1949, the National Party has been voted into power, and the elaborate legislation of formalised apartheid is on the drawing board – legislation that will lead, amongst many other things, to the destruction of Cato Manor itself and the forced removal of its approximately 180 000 inhabitants. Yet, despite his awareness of racial 'marking' and prioritising of space ('the Jew's shop', 'the white area' and 'the Indian area') in Dumisane's gaze, it is the white gardeners who are alien and 'other' in the landscape. In a story set a few years earlier, two young Indian boys claim identity and belonging in the intimately known and named place as they live out their child-heroic fantasies:

> Cherry Lane was at the base of the triangle that bordered bus owner Moodley's opulent abode, joining Trimborne Road and Rathmines. A sandy footpath separated Moodley's large plot from the empty no-man's land that sloped down to the valley. There was a single, well-climbed mango tree on this no-man's land – the look-out post of some pirate ship adrift on a sea of long grass, making dreamy waves in the autumn winds. Before he was a boxing champion, Nunda was the captain of the pirate ship while Boywa was Robinson Crusoe. Nunda's pirate ship soon ran aground and Robinson Crusoe eventually found his way back to civilisation. Time has a way of changing the scenario – the fantasies quite often remaining.
>
> And so the pirate became Joe *The Brown Bomber* Louis and Robinson Crusoe, that other renowned pugilist, Joe *Manassa Mauler* Dempsey. (54–55)

In *'At the Edge' and Other Cato Manor Stories*, Ronnie Govender offers a series of narratives of life in Cato Manor from the 1940s until its destruction in 1958–59. Against the strict delineation of identity, the control of space, a state narrative of racial separation and displacement, and an official cartography (of race and economics), Govender sets an unofficial cartography of knowing, belonging and growing, a stature in ordinary character, an oral-influenced mobility of storytelling, a carnivalesque chorus of voices and the ingenuity of tactic – as well as the desolation of suffering and destruction that was to follow the bulldozing of Cato Manor and the forced removal of its residents. While the stories deal specifically with the destruction of Cato Manor, they resonate with larger claims about South African Indian identities without simply essentialising or valorising them, and without constructing them as identities of exclusion or glossing over areas of difficulty or prejudice. Questions of alienation, belonging, immigration, rootedness, exclusion, exoticism and indigeneity swirl through the narrative landscape of the collection.

* * *

Govender was born in Cato Manor in 1934, one of ten siblings. As well as encountering oral storytelling through his mother and grandmother, he became interested in theatre after seeing André Huguenet's performance in *Oedipus Rex* while he was still at school. He was educated at Springfield Teachers' Training College, and worked at various times as a teacher, a part-time journalist (he was sports editor for *The Leader*) and for the South African Breweries. He was involved in the South African Council on Sport (Sacos), and later in the Congress of South African Writers (Cosaw). Govender also formed Durban's Shah Theatre Academy, and was active in community theatre, establishing a name for himself as a playwright. His productions include: *The Lahnee's Pleasure*; *Swami*; *Off-Side!*; *In-Side!*; *Blossoms from the Bough*; *At the Edge*; and *1949* (the last two based largely on a number of stories in *'At the Edge' and Other Cato Manor Stories*). He served as the director of the Playhouse Company in Durban, and currently works in a communications company in Cape Town.

'At the Edge' and Other Cato Manor Stories was published in 1996. The setting of the stories themselves ranges from the 1940s through the 1950s. Govender states in the Introduction: 'I began writing these stories after my family moved from Cato Manor in the fifties, when the district became the first victim of the National Party's notorious Group Areas Act' (11). The blurb on the back cover of the book says: 'Nobody had ventured to explore the lives, tragedies and patois of the Indian communities in South Africa until Ronnie wrote these stories in the sixties'. Nevertheless, the date of the writing or rewriting of some of the stories is clearly later than this, as indicated by references to watching television (which was introduced to South Africa in the early 1970s), television games (which arrived in the early 1980s or so), and the 'current rap hit number, *Pump Up The Jam!*' (95–96) (which was only released by the band Technotronic in 1990). The predominantly retrospective cast to the narrative voice suggests a memorialisation of place: a reclaiming of place and one's rights to live (in) it through the articulation of voice and community. Something of the purpose of the collection is suggested by Govender in the Prologue: 'Listen, my friends, listen to the voices of Cato Manor, District Six and Sophiatown as we struggle to fashion a new life – a life free from the contradictions that prevent us from seeing God in Everyman' (16). The mythologising impulse, evident here in the linking of Cato Manor with two sites of removal that have been extensively valorised in popular discourse, is offset by a specificity of reference to the Cato Manor community and its infrastructure in the Introduction, a specificity carried through in the stories themselves:

> In the thirties the Cato Manor community began building its own schools, shops and bazaars, temples, churches and mosques, and set up welfare institutions such as the now nationally established home for orphans and the aged, the Aryan Benevolent Home. They even provided their own bus service and built a crematorium and social and sporting amenities, while paying the same rates and taxes as Durban's white

> citizens. They achieved this at a time when unemployment was endemic and tuberculosis rife.
>
> A survey by the University of Natal in the fifties revealed that over eighty per cent of the community was living below the breadline. Yet it went on to establish itself as a vibrant, viable community from which emerged many outstanding people – political activists George Sewpersadh, president of the Natal Indian Congress, N.T. Naicker, Bennie Bunsee and Sister Poomanie, trade unionists R.D. Naidu and Billy Peters who represented South Africa at the first Communist Internationale, educationists Bernard Barnabas, Y.G. Reddy and Jack Naidoo, who was the first black rector of the M.L. Sultan Technikon, transport tycoons J. Seebran and M.M. Reddy, hoteliers Chin Govender, the Bughwandeen brothers and M.N. Reddy, furniture manufacturer D. Pardesi, South African boxing champions Jack Govender, Frank Moodley and Sonny Govender, journalists Gonny Govender, formerly of *Drum* and the BBC, author and now editor of the London based *Asian Times*, Ticks Chetty, the former *Sunday Times* Durban bureau chief and Dennis Pather, editor of the *Daily News*, cultural leaders Mathiemugan and Swamivel Pillay, Rookmoney Naidoo and Jugadesan Devar, sports administrators Charles Pillay and Sooboo Rajah, weight-lifter Sunny Moodley, along with many others who were pioneers of the sports boycott, and numerous other distinguished men and women. (11–12)

As the title of the collection makes clear, the term 'the edge' is key to the volume's concerns, and its valencies are complex. The blurb on the inside cover gives 'the edge' a socio-political turn: 'the backdrop for these tales is Cato Manor during the forties, fifties and sixties[2] – at the edge of apartheid upheavals in South Africa'; and there are constant references in the stories to the control of spatiality and movement by apartheid legislation. The title story induces a (Hindu) religious understanding of the term:

> *Aaleyel sothie yen, ambale thaado woorm*
> *Maalet seelam badi vazh thi vanaguvaam*
> 'You whose light is measureless and who dances in the Amabalam's gaze
> We bow at thy flower-bedecked anklets and crave thy blessings'
>
> Have we not been brought to the edge by such musing, to the edge of reason where perhaps lies our true nature? Have we not then touched that peace we are restless for, tasted the waters of an undying stillness from which our souls yearn to drink forever? (61);

and:

> She abused the heavens for their cruelty. Why should she be punished so? She sat in her temple for days, overcome by grief and anger, demanding an explanation. And then one day, in the stillness the song rose from within her . . .
>
> *Woolegalam woonen thothet kareeavan* . . .
>
> And she was at the edge.
>
> At the edge . . . where life meant something else, something far removed from what she had known and felt. She knew then that God did not want to hear her anger and that there was greater peace in prayer than she had known. (62)

In the very next story, 'Saris, Bangles and Bees', the term means something rather different:

> Durban's humidity had an upsetting effect. The turgid, sticky heat clung to your beleaguered skin and rivulets of sweat would flow through your hair and over your eyes till you

> were on edge. There was little you could do beside wipe away the sweat and seek the shade of some leafy tree, which wasn't very helpful if there wasn't any breeze blowing. (65)

Despite the fact that 'the edge' is a term or concept that appears infrequently, and then rather ambiguously, the stories themselves constantly explore 'edges' – approach them, move over them, and at times reinforce them. They evoke a place and a community itself on the edge of official Durban, and soon to be edged out, but also comprising numerous internal edges (religious, racial, linguistic, economic and social), and pushing at both internal and external edges. The stories negotiate internal and external liminalities in a way far removed from metropolitan postcolonial thinking. While writers such as Salman Rushdie or Michael Ondaatje, or critics such as Homi Bhabha or Gayatri Chakravorty Spivak, celebrate their status as intellectual migrants,[3] Govender's characters experience boundaries as sticky sweat, religious faith, barbed wire and forced removals. We are reminded that the postcolonial in the 'South' is primarily a matter of conditions of survival, rather than a metaphorical or allegorical space of hybrid freedom.[4]

* * *

The opening 'narrative' of the collection is a hand-drawn map of Cato Manor.[5] It has, in the list of contents, the same status as a story, and is metonymic, or perhaps metaphorical, of the larger concerns, and form, of the volume: in a sense it is the 'map' to all the stories. While 'accurate' in terms of street names and geographical location, its markers and icons are distinct from those of official cartography. It is a mapping of character, theme and use (Cut-Neck-Bobby's House, Ahmed's Shop, Vellama's House, Adam's Garage, Ahmedia Mosque and Bus Owner Moodley's House), and of inclusion and exclusion (White School, Municipal Housing for Indians, Westridge Park Coloured Sports Ground, Cato Manor Hindu Cemetery and Muslim Cemetary [*sic*]). Simon Ryan points out that '[h]istorically, maps and other cartographic representations have served as symbolic icons of power' (1994: 116), and that mapping is a process by which 'the land itself is inserted into a particular narrativisation of history . . . [T]he cartographic inscriptions are not simply reflections of reality but organise and license the appropriation and exploitation of the land' (1994: 127). Cartography connects 'textual and material vectors of colonialism': 'An inscription on a map is in some senses performative. As a plan it licenses material construction, and also monumentalises that same construction' (1994: 128). Drawing attention to the textual and performative – rather than the natural/empirical – status of cartography allows the possibility of contesting cartographies: this is precisely Govender's project (and Douglas Livingstone's?). Ryan points out that '[t]o posit the land as a text is to claim its readability, and thence to arrogate power over it', and that 'politically . . . the map acts as an incitement to the alteration of ownership' (1994: 126). In opposition to the official apartheid map on which Cato Manor was identified as an un-differentiated black space requiring erasure, Govender offers the nuanced and named place, known in its history and intimate detail – what Gunner refers to as a '"thick" sense of place' (1996: 123). His project in this is analogous to the spatial, as opposed to imperial, history proposed for Australia by Paul Carter in *The Road to Botany Bay* (1987): a 'prehistory of places, a history of roads, footprints, trails of dust and foaming waves' (Darian-Smith et al. 1996: 5). As Gunner says in relation to another context: 'In the aesthetics of naming . . . the land frequently becomes the person, and becomes part of the body's text; the social and the historical self is perceived through the land' (1996: 120).

The informal, yet compelling, mapping of place finds its textual correlative in the looser, oral-influenced narrative style. The Foreword to the collection stresses the oral origin of the stories: 'Ronnie spent his entire youth in Cato Manor, with his mother and grandmother spinning masterful stories for him and his siblings. His interest in theatre and storytelling was certainly fuelled by the impression these childhood stories made on him' (13). There are numerous references to oral storytelling in the narratives themselves, as in this example from the story 'Poobathie' in which the old widow Vellama tells stories:

> [S]he taught the children all the little rituals and told them fascinating stories about Marriammen, the goddess.
>
> 'Once, many, many years ago, after the first white people came, there was a small-pox epidemic in India . . .' (27);

and this from the story 'The Cosmic Clash':

> And that was Sathie's cue to tell them his favourite story. He didn't ever tell them that he was a lousy marble player. Of course . . . he didn't lie. He just didn't tell them. To some extent he did say it like it was; to an extent. One had to make allowances for some lapses in memory because it happened a long time ago.
>
> Here then is the real story . . . (96)

There are also references to oral histories, handed down from parents to children and other family members:

> While he was hazy about historical details, he remembered what his father had said, again and again. The turbaned old man had said it to his mother, hoe in hand, side-by-side in their market garden and he said it to his friends and relatives on family occasions and festivals, especially when the occasional nip of cane spirits burned its way through the walls of his stomach.
>
> 'The Dravidians, the Shaivites were the natives of India. They lived in Mohenjodaro and Harrappa in the north of India until the Aryans, who were war-like barbarians, invaded them and pushed them south. They were highly civilised and taught the world to count.' (85)

In form, the stories in the collection are punctuated by oral markers. Many open with the kind of conversational remarks with which an oral narrator would preface his or her story. For example: 'There was a scarcity of rice in those days and you were something of a big shot if you had rice served in your house. Mealie-rice wasn't all that bad if you knew how to cook it' (37). In certain of the stories, the narrative structure is circular, as is evident in so many oral forms; and narrative linkages and disjunctures depend, for the most part, on techniques of performative storytelling: parallel formulations ('Once while playing rounders . . . Once Poobathie asked the old lady' [28]); the dramatic introduction of a specific event ('there was never any violence until that particular evening' [42]); second-person address to the hearer/reader ('so, you see, death . . .' [84]); or a cyclical linking back to the opening or repeated theme. As in the Oom Schalk Lourens stories of Herman Charles Bosman, or the bar-room stories of Damon Runyon, in which the narrator may assume the oral storyteller's prerogative of stepping outside the narrative to comment on its implications or on his own narration, Govender's narrators often include their own perceptions:

> Isn't it a pity that the professional mourner has gone out of business – made extinct by the impact of Western culture – so-called? Nowadays some alienated souls frown on what they call 'mawkish and sentimental' funerals, but is it not better to cry your heart out, than to eat your heart out, simply because you want to appear refined? Is it not a kind of perversity to punish yourself so, when you can lean on someone's shoulder to try to lessen the grief of death, a grief not totally beyond human solace? (84)

Elsewhere the narrator comments: 'How times have changed . . . Nowadays people waste food. Those days life was hard' (38).

While drawing on older forms of storytelling, the orality is very much that of a community of modernity, shaped by media such as radio and television (what Ong calls secondary orality, but which I see instead as tertiary orality[6]). The 'ethnic' imperatives of the South African Broadcasting Corporation (SABC) under the previous government notwithstanding, radio is a widely heard voice in the Cato Manor community:

> Ruthnam Pillay would be introducing the Indian programme on SABC and every radio in the district would be turned on full blast . . . Ruthnam Pillay's very Indian accent, especially chosen by the very white SABC, would be heard from Cato Manor Road to Second River, and further, 'Good morning listeners, *vanakum*, *namaaste* and *salaams* to you very good people.' (66)

Cinema and jazz music also provide modes of narration and expression, as does the introduction of television, especially in the retrospective framing narrative of the story 'The Cosmic Clash', in which a marble game between children is recast in terms of comedic caricature, superheroes and special effects:

> As far as he was concerned age hadn't diminished Sathie's histrionic talents. He brought vividly to life all the little details, or so he thought, of his childhood experiences in Cato Manor, replete with sound effects and action for the benefit of his wide-eyed grandchildren. Having been reared on the bathos and astonishing mimicry of those legends of the comic, Charlie Chaplin and N.S. Krishnan, he touched off his performances with just the right effects from today's hi-tech entertainment industry . . . he would simulate the action on TV: 'Bang! Bang! Rat-a-tat-tat!' with machine guns, AK 47s, rayguns blazing. He would switch to a karate chop, 'Aiyaaa!' and then turn into a space vehicle, 'Zoom!' and finally a few strident bars from the current rap hit number, *Pump up the Jam!* (95–96)

As well as linking an intimate cartography of knowing with the form of oral-influenced narrative, the stories claim belonging through an emotionally charged evocation of the built and natural worlds. The constant references to architecture and vegetation in the stories, almost in their repeated patternings having the status of oral formulae, give foundation and root to the claims to place. Hofmeyr points out that building on and working deeply into the soil were central to colonial notions of occupation:

> This idea of height and depth was extremely important to colonial understandings of land possession. African agriculture, for example, was considered derisory largely because it was seen as 'shallow'. Colonial farmers, on the other hand, ploughed 'deeply' and so apparently possessed – and earned a right to – the land in a way quite distinct from African farmers. In the perception of the Native Affairs Department, Africans did not 'love the soil' which under their 'scratching' became 'thin' and 'bodiless'. Europeans, on the other hand, practised 'good husbandry' and made the soil 'thick' by adding manure and fertiliser. Alongside this folkloric language, the more scientific vocabularies of geology and surveying also embody notions of possession. Both these disciplines generate the illusion of a saturated knowledge of the earth that stretches both horizontally and vertically. (1993: 72)

Govender's stories clearly counter accusations of Africans/Indians living place in a 'thin' sense. The poem which serves as the Epilogue, entitled 'Cato Manor', comprises precisely what Gunner calls 'the poetry of the peopled land' (1996: 121):

> beneath the heaving crowns of mango
> flowers bearing the promise of a child's summer
> the games we played
> the friendships we forged

the battles we fought
and the love we made
beneath those heaving crowns
of mango flowers. (157)

Vegetation abounds in the stories: 'chanting under the quilt of leaves on the spreading boughs of the huge syringa tree near the temple' (30); 'standing under the syringa tree nibbling at the *prasad*' (34); 'The yellowing syringa leaves floated down and settled on the old lady's hair' (35); 'The designated tree, a huge jack-fruit tree, stood in a clearing among the tombstones' (50); 'She kept a small temple at the back of the house, singing *thevarams* under the syringa tree. They were making beds for dhania, herbs and brinjal' (72); 'the sounds rising gently to caress the quilt of leaves on the spreading boughs of the syringa tree' (61); '[Bees] buzzed aggressively over the flowers and to and from the hole in the Umdoni tree where they were building their honeycomb' (65); 'someone should collect the honey from the Umdoni tree' (73); 'He was standing alongside his bougainvillea hedge which he was pruning . . . (105); 'His *skafing* spot was behind the overgrown hedge of Thumba's yard fronting Discovery Road. An umdoni tree and some banana plants provided cover' (131); 'Most of Mayville/Cato Manor was covered in sub-tropical growth, but the cemetery area had been cleared of trees and the silhouettes of the tombstones stood out starkly against the sky' (131); and 'he was there among the ink-berry bushes, the guava trees and the reeds' (120).

As well as evoking vividly a sense of place, vegetation intrudes into the narrating and/or focalising consciousnesses: 'For all the sinew on his tiny frame, Boywa might have been a bamboo in China's yard . . .' (53); or: 'Girls were forbidden fruit, in the Tamil vernacular – the allure of the sun-ripened, spotless, juicy mango . . .' (132).

With a few exceptions, the plants evoked above are exotics that have been imported into South Africa. However, crucially they become a means of claiming an indigenised identity. In a story that deals with the 1949 riots, 'Call of the Muezzin', in which African people attacked Indian people, claiming, amongst other things, that they had no rights of belonging, the African focaliser talks of the journey of these plants to the South African landscape, and their 'naturalness', in a way that suggests a shift into the concerns of the authorial consciousness. The indigenisation of these plants, rooted now in the soil of Cato Manor and shaping its lived character, both echoes and guarantees that of their planters:

> The Umkumbaan cut a swathe through Cato Manor's lush sub-tropica and market gardens brimming with vegetables, paw-paw, avocado, mango, guava, jack fruit, curry leaf and other exotic plants brought over from India in the nineteenth century by indentured labourers. It was miraculous how these plants survived the months' long journey in those rickety sailing vessels and subsequent planting in a foreign clime. Whites who lived over the Berea ridge called the plants 'exotic', but to Elias and his Cato Manor fellows the pungent aroma of the curry leaf mingling with the subtle almost musk-like wisps from mango flowers or the tantalising smell of ripening jack fruit was as natural as daylight. (120–21)

In the same story, Cato Manor residents vegetate the landscape in more intimate (and humorous) ways:

> The pungent aroma of ripe guavas enveloped him and he had to avoid squashing the fallen over-ripe fruit underfoot. Amazing the kids hadn't raided the trees the way they had done when he and his mates were kids. In his day there wouldn't have been a single, ripe guava left. People's habits were changing fast. How sad! What was the world coming to when children stopped climbing trees?
>
> He remembered the time when there wasn't a single guava tree in Booth Road. How did they get there? He knew how, even though he tried hard not to remember. When you're a child it's okay. Children are innocent. Such thoughts in adults

> are haram. Still, the memories pushed through the heavy veil of moral censure and he recalled with uncontrollable fits of giggling, how after stuffing himself on the lovely guavas his cousins had brought from Clairwood on Eid Day, he was forced to relieve himself in the bushes at the very same spot where he was now standing. Ahmed had teased him that a guava tree would grow on the spot where his little load of naturally manured guava seeds lay. Indeed, several months later a few guava trees had sprung up at that exact same spot. Nature was wonderful. He was deep in guava memory land when Elias ran out of the store. (125)

Within the vegetation are the 'neat wood-and-iron homes' of the Cato Manor residents (the phrase is a constantly repeated refrain):

> All the money would go towards rebuilding the old wood-and-iron house Basdeo had inherited from his late father. It had been a solidly built structure nestling amongst avocado, mango and flamboyant trees, a pretty garden filled with different varieties of pride-of-India, carnations and roses with lush granadilla creepers and golden shower shrubs adorning the fences on either side. (78)

The care taken in the construction and upkeep of the buildings, as well as their inhering within, rather than being imposed upon, the landscape is central to Govender's insistence on the viability and value of the Cato Manor community, and consequently the extreme brutality of its destruction: the 'neat', 'smart' buildings 'stand below' (26–27) or 'nestle among' (101) trees and plants that are lovingly named and bounteous in shade or fruit.

The landscape is peopled by an array of lively characters, and the interaction between them constitutes much of the interest and narrative 'work' of the collection. As well as having affinities with the stories of Bosman and Runyon, in their adaptation of oral techniques to the printed form, Govender's narratives are in many ways (his)stories from below, akin to those of José Luandino Vieira, which make their meaning to a large extent through dialogue, evoking the voices of individuals in community. The fact of the narratives' ready adaptation to the stage testifies to the importance of dramatic interchanges in them.

As De Certeau and Giard point out:

> Orality . . . constitutes the essential space of community. In a society, there is no communication without orality, even when this society gives a large place to what is written for the memorising of tradition or the circulation of knowledge. Social exchange demands a correlation of gestures and bodies, a presence of voices and accents, marks of breathing and passions, an entire hierarchy of complementary information necessary for interpreting a message that goes beyond a simple statement – rituals of address and greeting, chosen registers of expression, nuances added by intonation, facial movements. It must have this *vocal grain* through which the speaker becomes identified and individualised, and this way of making a visceral, fundamental link between sound, meaning, and body. (1998: 252)

They talk of the 'sonorous materiality' of exchanged speech (1998: 253), claiming: 'A city breathes when *places for speech* exist within it, regardless of their official function – the neighbourhood café, the marketplace, the line at the post office, the newspaper stand, or the main door of the school at the end of the day' (1998: 253–54).

Govender's stories explore precisely this 'vocal grain', the 'places for speech' in which a 'cuisine of gestures and words' (De Certeau and Giard 1998: 254) is prepared and consumed. The dialogue is nuanced in its exploration of relations between characters themselves, and between characters and their social environment, and Govender uses dialect or patois (he employs both terms in interviews in explaining his dramatic/narrative mode) in a manner similar to that of his plays (in particular *The Lahnee's Pleasure*). In the story

'Brothers of the Spirit', for example, questions of poverty, class prejudice, gender relations and sexual morality are enacted in a conversation between Cut-Neck-Bobby's parents:

> 'Ram, no oil. I told you, no oil!'
> 'No oil, no oil, no this, no that. Money falls from trees, what?'
> 'How I must cook then?'
> 'Why you use so much oil?'
> 'When you saw me using lot oil? Next door, Salatchi's husband make sure they got enough groceries. I must shout everyday.'
> 'Muthu's working for the factory. You think he's better than me because I work in the garden . . .?'
> 'I never say he's better than you, but he gives Salatchi everything and . . . and . . . he don't go to Mehmoon's house . . .'
> 'You saw me going to Mehmoon's house?'
> 'Everytime you see that Mehmoon you go way funny. Big man like you, you smile, you so nice. But with me every time you quiet like one mouse.'
> 'Mustn't smile at anybody. I'm asking you, mustn't smile at anybody?'
> 'Why don't you smile at me then . . . why you only smile at that Mehmoon. You not her husband . . .' (40)

In commenting on his own practice, Govender is concerned to distinguish legitimate uses of patois/dialect from those that are ignorant or insulting:

> It was necessary to take patois out of its private life, self-conscious domain and confer legitimacy beyond the proscenium arch, once the preserve of the malleable middle class, badgered into soulless conformity by a dominant culture . . . However, it was inevitable that once the torch had been lit, many false bearers would attempt to carry it out of sheer opportunism. Once it was demonstrated, as *The Lahnee's*

Pleasure did with overwhelming success, that patois would strike ready chord in its audience, the vultures moved in and exploited it for commercial gain, as, I am afraid, they are still doing. A spate of mediocre plays have since debased patois to the point of ethnic ridicule, caricaturing accents rather than capturing speech patterns and turns of phrase and by appealing to the lowest common denominator for laughs. In our culture of racial and ethnic stereotyping, this vulgar practice continues without compunction even in advertising in documentaries and soaps on national television and radio. I once turned down an invitation to write sequences for the local television soap opera *Generations* because the leading Coloured and Indian characters were stereotyped as either money-hungry swindlers or as hopeless drunks.

The challenge is to contextualise this adaptation of language in such a way that in speaking from the heart its innate dignity and power transcends the barriers which, ironically, English as a tool of imperialism had created. There is also the tendency when dealing with patois to confuse language with accents. Some accents are easy on the ear, some are difficult to comprehend and some are funny. If you listen to the accents of a Welsh speaker of English and that of an earlier generation of South African Indians, there is not much of a difference. Yet unlike the Indian accent, the Welsh accent is not perceived as being funny. Local white comedians have often, with sadistic delight, shored up their pathetic repertoires with very broadly caricatured Applesamy and Naidoo accents.

Dialects, however, bring a dimension to language that often enhances that language and can therefore have a literary legitimacy. In the metaphor of the patois there are charming turns of phrase which reflect warm familiarity and intimacy as with such sincere invitations as: 'Howzit bro, let's vie pozzie and catch a chow'. A playwright of integrity avoids

> playing to the gallery and appealing to the lowest common denominator. There are those, however, who use an accent that is looked upon as belonging to the lower classes and exploit it for the sake of cheap laughs. The problem is that legitimate, skilful and honest usage of patois is unfortunately lumped in with the former. (Chetty 2002: 338–39)[7]

Such observations support Rajend Mesthrie's extensive and sophisticated analysis of South African Indian Englishes (1992a; 1992b), in particular their historical and class shadings, and the complexities of syntax and vocabulary that are involved – far removed from the parodic versions of white comedians. Govender particularly uses language to explore behaviour patterns enforced by apartheid, in the contrasting of 'legitimate, skilful and honest usage of patois' with the self-deprecatory, and strategic, 'Applesamy' mode adopted for whites in authority:

> [H]e would sell his wares to the white madams, most of whom had grown quite fond of their efficient and reliable vendor, Sammy, although they had never really bothered to find out what his real name was . . .
>
> 'Fresh dhania, Madam, fresh carrots, big, big cabbages . . .' and under his breath he would mumble whenever one of the madams bought dhania, 'Arreh, what these people know about dhania? They don't know nothing about jeera or garam masala. Cultured people eat cultured food. They only eat kowtchi food – meat, boiled meat all the time. What they know about food? What they know about anything? That's why they frightened for us, they don't want to give us a chance. If I only get one shop there by Fenniscowles Road – if only they give me a chance, I'll show them . . .'
>
> But he was a wise Sammy. Or so he thought, as he kept his feelings to himself and smiled graciously at the madams.
>
> 'Hello Madam, hello Madam. How's Madam's corns today? No the ones on your toes. Still paining? Oh shame. Madam

> must put manja. My house anything happens we put manja, where doctor and all that! Can't afford it. What's manja? Oh, that yellow thing you put in the curry. How you say . . . turmeric powder, that's right. You know, Madam, my son, the eldest fullah, stupid fullah, he cut his leg with one broke milk bottle . . . thava big cut, no zaggeration. We put manja, put manja, thava no time got better. Must use manja, Madam. What, Madam? Cabbages? For you only sixpence. What, two cabbages? Lo-o-vely, Madam, thank you, thank you.' (39)

The use of dialect here serves not to caricature or ridicule, but to evoke a resilience, warmth and liveliness of identity and community.

There are, nevertheless, dangers, as Govender acknowledges, and as writers from contexts as diverse as Ireland and the Caribbean have discovered: at what point, and for whom, does the 'authentic' recreation of speech patterns become parodic? In the case of *'At the Edge' and Other Cato Manor Stories*, there are certain humorous interchanges such as the following which, were they penned by a white author, would likely be considered racist or degrading:

> 'Hare' Maaaire'! You broke my head!'
> 'I never break it, I poked it!'
> Bolwa's wife screamed hysterically at the gathering neighbours, 'Call the police, call the police! They poking my husband . . . they murdering him!' (45)

This takes us to the heart of contentious debates about representation and 'speaking for'. As is so often the case, the answer seems to return to intentionality and the right to speak: like African Americans using the term 'nigger' to address each other, or Indian people using 'charou' as a term of ironic affection or recognition, the question must be framed: who is using the term/mode of speech and for what purpose?

Despite Govender's extensive, and in my opinion largely effective, use of dialect/patois in evoking and exploring a sense of individuals in community, there is a slightly problematic aspect to the diction. Particularly, though not exclusively, in the voice of the narrator, some readers may be struck by what appear to be slightly archaic or inappropriately classical usages: a 'jol' is attended by some 'timid chaps' (43); the darkness at one point is 'stygian' (51); boxing is in the same paragraph 'the noble art' and 'the blood-thirsty sport' (53); a dog is described as 'vent[ing] his romantic ardours' (79); a character who has just raped a girl says 'I feel like a heel' (136); and the poem that comprises the Epilogue includes a reference to 'the hallowed turf of Mayville Ground' (158). It is unclear to what extent this unevenness of diction reflects patterns of usage in the Cato Manor community, influenced in part by colonial/apartheid schooling, Govender's own slighty erratic choices of language, or even a self-consciousness 'literariness'.

* * *

The lively and nuanced speech in the stories is crucial to the evocation of character in community, but it is the characters themselves who constitute Govender's most powerful statement of belonging, identification and resistance: in opposition to the undifferentiated mass faced with forced removal, Govender offers the particularity of life, character and identity.[8] The collection builds up a sense of community through characters who recur from one story to the next, and whose homes or places of work are frequently located on the map that comprises the frontispiece. Govender himself says: 'Although I have taken some poetic licence in the telling, these stories are based on the lives of the people who lived in Cato Manor and deal with actual experiences, such as the 1949 riots and an exorcism performed by my grandmother' (12). The characters are often vividly named, and placed within a community of meaning, significance and relationship:

> To get back to Premlall; they called him Cut-Neck-Bobby, because in the words of a schoolfriend, 'He was so thick you could hardly see his neck.'

> You see, he was a stubby character with fat jowls which hid his rather short neck and when he turned his head his whole body turned with it.
>
> Cut-Neck-Bobby had developed into a heavy drinker over the years, although he never stumbled or measured the road like Bullwa did when *he* was drunk. Bullwa was a real bull of a man who never smiled. They lived, with their families, in a wood-and-iron house . . . in Cato Manor Road which separated the Indian area from the white suburb of the Berea. (41)

Several characters seem to expand beyond the pettiness or degradation of their surroundings:

> Everything Paw-Paw did he did in a big way. He could pick up an entire car engine with his bare hands . . . I actually saw him do it. He loved sour porridge. He would pick three or four green chillies from Vellama's garden, rinse them under the tap and chew them as if they were the tastiest morsels he had ever eaten. He would then wash them down with a huge jug of sour porridge which Vellama would make for him every time he helped her son-in-law, Jack, fix up motor cars. He would polish off the jug in one mighty draught, after which he would smack his lips and get back to work.
>
> 'Hey, Jack, gimme 'nother one engine there!' (47)

Others reveal the heroism of ordinary survival, such as Ayakanoo who – in his job of emptying toilet buckets – seeks dignity in his determination 'to become the best bucket carrier around' (71); or a vividness of emotional or intellectual response, such as the barman Thaver in the story 'The Incomplete Human Being', who teaches Tamil, quotes extensively from memory from the Tholkapium, and accompanies *raags* on the violin. Throughout the narratives, the characters wrestle with the divisions of class, religion and gender in ways that are compelling: 'The children were growing. They could not afford to feed, clothe and educate them on his meagre earnings. That convinced Harry. He was a firm believer in good education, for the boys' (29); 'if your father's name was not Pillay, Reddy, Singh, Maharaj or even Mohamed, you didn't feature in the consciousness of people' (25); 'Charles! Not only was he a Christian, he was also low caste' (33); 'Then there was Billy's wife, Gonum, stuck at home with seven children to care for, and a market garden to look after while every now and then Billy sneaked off to his Coloured mistress, Putuus' (69); 'As it turned out she had no say in her marriage. It was all arranged by her parents and the only time she saw the boy was in the *pundal*' (71); and 'Basdeo and she had a long argument about the name, "Why do you insist on giving the dog a white name? We are not whites. Why can't we call the dog Kunthi, or Poolmanthie, or something like that?"' (80)

There is also extensive and detailed exploration of African/Indian interaction and animosity in the two stories that deal specifically with the events of 1949 ('1949' and 'Call of the Muezzin . . . To a Slow Samba Beat'). Even in the final story which treats at length resistance to the destruction of Cato Manor, a lively and unusual human perspective is evident in the attempt of a son to prevent his father from engaging in what he perceives to be futile opposition:

> Devan was angry, 'Appa, this is absolute stupidity. Who do you think you are, Mahatma Gandhi? Everybody's moved out, even those people who made all those inspiring speeches at the Mayville Theatre. Do you think that one man is going to change things? You are causing undue pain to Amma. You have no right to do this. Don't you care for your family?'
>
> 'No, I don't care for my family. That's why I battled so you could have a roof over your head. You are lucky. When I was fifteen, I didn't have shoes.' (154)

The characters remain a persistent presence long after the stories have been read – as they, their real-life counterparts, or their descendants remain a powerful living and shaping presence within the Durban region and beyond, in spite of the destruction of Cato Manor.

* * *

I have referred approvingly above to the oral-influenced form of the stories. One aspect of their structure is nevertheless troubling. Many end on what appears to be a note of bathos or triviality. 'Lala Phansi' moves through a lively evocation of the ingenuity of character and tactic, an unexpected and then double plot reversal, to end with the line, 'You can bet your life that Sonny-Boy always paid his parking fines after that' (23), which seems unintentionally to trivialise its implications. The story 'The Incomplete Human Being' undertakes a complex analysis of cultural change and identity formation, focusing on the issue of linguistic/religious instruction in a context of modernity and cross-cultural encounter. Yet the narrative ends with an articulation of essentialism that appears to work precisely against the paradox and shift that the story evokes: 'Now in his sixties, a retired school principal, Sathie would often recall Mr Taver's caustic metaphor, his dire warning of cultural disintegration, and he regretted not just his own halting Tamil, but that none of his children or grandchildren could speak their own tongue . . . *the world's oldest living language*' (94). There are many other such examples, all of which seem to me awkwardly to apply a trite closure to stories that themselves resist simple conclusion.

It is difficult to account for this. Does Govender find himself as author wrenched – in finding endings for his narratives – from the 'open-endedness' of the oral narrative to the closure which he feels print requires? Or, contrastingly, is he responding to what he regards as the moral imperative of the oral folktale? Is he offering the 'take-home message' which so much popular fiction and drama seems to require?[9] Is Govender, as an author who is well trained in script writing, utilising a convention evident in theatre from Shakespeare to *Woza Albert!*, of concluding with something memorable (installing a new king, raising political martyrs) but which – in the spectacle of performance – does not need to answer the questions raised by the play itself: a convention which does not translate well into the short story form? In partial rebuttal of this suggestion, but perhaps indicating his own dissatisfaction with the endings, Govender omitted the final (and to me bathetic) lines of the story 'Lala Phansi' in the performance of the play *1949* which he staged in 2004 at the Centre for African Literary Studies at the University of KwaZulu-Natal.

* * *

The narrator of the story 'Brothers of the Spirit', Cut-Neck-Bobby, whose name features prominently near the top of the map, says:

> There was a host of haunting memories of a lifetime spent at the hearth of his *atman*: the soil he'd never imagine he'd be torn away from, the rich, red soil of Cato Manor.
>
> Nostalgia, however, is the hand-maiden of delusion. (38)

As with accounts of other places of forced removal, the danger remains of blurring memory into mythology; of creating a narrative of place and belonging that exists only in fictionalised imaginative terms, and which has little historical weight or particularity. The narratives of Govender's *'At the Edge' and Other Cato Manor Stories* present lives and identities that are geographically located and legislatively displaced, accommodating and yet often jealously guarding boundaries of religion, class and caste, juggling economic pragmatics and ethical principles, at once personally and socially resourceful and politically overwhelmed. Rooted as they are in the specificities of 1940s and 50s Durban South Africa, the stories continue to speak eloquently about South African Indian identities in the urban space, and indeed to the possibilities and restrictions of the postcolonial city, in its multiple forms.

6

'Who's that Black Boys Making that Black Noise Step a Little Closer to the Mic'

Prophets of da City and Urban (South African) Identity

I kick messages to society
But if you diss me you'll see
A totally different side of me.
A totally opposite side of the Prophet
There's no way you can stop it
When it gets catastrophic
I explode and drop the next load of rhymes
You mind and you find that the episode
Can't kick as I come equipped
To make sure that I hit
I won't quit

Don't stop, let the speakers pop
Just dance until you drop
Prophets of da City, 'Kickin' Non-Stop'

In this chapter I investigate expressions of identity and belonging in South African rap music, focusing specifically on the band Prophets of da City (POC). My concern is with the way in which identity is articulated, claimed and performed through lyrics, music, dance, style, and the associated activities of hip-hop culture, including graffiti or spray-can art. Writing critical accounts of performance forms always involves difficult questions of approach and methodology. Rap, in particular, is a form – mobile, shifting, yet with a long generic history; playful, irreverent, serious; challenging and confrontational, yet often deeply conservative; finding politics in pleasure – with its own very specific challenges for criticism. Part of the task of this chapter, then, is to find an approach and a form to deal with rap music. This approach and form need to have sufficient theoretical grounding to take up the necessary task of critical analysis, but be nimble enough for the mobilities and pleasures of the genre itself; they need to maintain the validity of academic enquiry, while subjecting the academy to challenge by voices outside of it – specifically here the rappers themselves whose response to those attempting institutional definition and control is often an aggressive 'FUCK OFF!'[1]

POC are one of the oldest, best-known and most prolific (some would add most influential) rap bands in South Africa. A consideration of their work takes us into a history of the form in South Africa, as well as the extent of its imbrication in senses of local identity for many young South Africans. POC have produced six albums to date: *Our World* (1990); *Boomstyle* (1992); *Age of Truth* (1993); *Phunk Phlow* (1994); *Universal Souljaz* (1995: United Kingdom and European release only); and *Ghetto Code* (1997). The latest album is apparently still in the production process.

From its inception the band has centred on Shaheen aka DSA (Shaheen Ariefdien) and Ready D aka DJ X-Plode (Deon Daniels), but membership has been as fluid as the musical form itself (the album credits indicate a blurring between the band itself and the larger POC crew/posse). At the time of the launch of the first album, the band also included Ramone (the group's dancer) and Jazmo (a beat boxer). Ramone left the band temporarily to be replaced by Junior 'Danisa' Dread on the third album (who left before the release of *Phunk Phlow*) and Ishmael Morabe. The first two albums contained rap mainly in English and Afrikaans, but Ishmael and Danisa have included Zulu and Xhosa. For the 1997 album, the band comprised Ready D, Ishmael, Shaheen, Mark (a breakdancer, and the youngest and newest member), and Ramone. More recently the line-up has changed again, with Shaheen leaving the band in 1999, and Ishmael focusing increasingly on his career as kwaito star E'Smile. Ready D is also involved with another rap band, Brasse vannie Kaap, and has an active career as a disc jockey (DJ).

POC have earned acclaim locally and internationally, though – like most rap bands – they have a thorny relationship with the media and recording industry. They have toured South Africa, Europe and America, playing amongst others at the Glastonbury festival and at Nelson Mandela's inauguration as president. They supported James Brown at the Brixton Academy, and British band Skunk Anansie on their South African tour. They have shared stages with Shabba Ranks, Afrika Bambaataa (with whom they also recorded a track), Public Enemy and The Fugees, and appeared with Liz Hurley and Ice Cube in the 1996 film *Dangerous Ground*.[2] Their single 'Neva Again' was nominated as single of the week by *New Musical Express*, and featured on the magazine's 1995 compilation album, the first South African act to be featured in this way. POC received the First National Bank South African music award for best rap album in 1995 for *Phunk Phlow*, and won the 1997 Cannes/Midem Award for best video for 'Understand Where I'm Coming From'. Despite such recognition and critical acclaim, POC's albums and videos have been consistently banned by the South African Broadcasting Corporation's (SABC) radio and television services, either for political content or expletives, and the band complains constantly, and it seems with justification, about a lack of support from their record company. (The credits on their first album end: 'We will change the industry for the better. There are far too many norms.') Like a great number of rap artists locally and internationally, POC have remained with an independent record label, Ghetto Ruff, through which they also record and promote other rap and kwaito artists, including Skeem, D'Low, Brasse vannie Kaap, 4FT Deep, Odameester, E'Smile and Mister Devious, though the distribution of the band's music has from the outset been handled by major companies (initially Teal, then Tusk, and now Polygram). POC's British record label is the independent Beggars Banquet. There have been more promising developments in recent years, with increased support for rap artists from record labels such as Polygram and greater airtime offered by South African radio stations.

* * *

> With vice I hold the mike device
> With force I keep it away of course
> And I'm keepin' you from sleepin'
> And on the stage I rage
> And I'm rollin'
> To the poor, I pour it on in metaphors
> Not bluffin', it's nothin'
> We ain't did before.
> *Public Enemy, 'Prophets of Rage'*

> I was out there dancing just to put bread on the table . . . Then later I started to practise with the turntable, day-in, day-out. At the weekends we'd take the hi-fi out into the road and dance. Then, later on, I'd have 20 to 30 people in our little home and neighbours would start banging on the walls. My mother found it nerve-wracking.
> *Ready D (Rouse 1995)*

Rap is a musical form that involves the rhythmic performance of words to a distinct – usually bass-heavy – beat. Though it is now often digitally sampled, the beat was originally created by dextrous manipulation of a vinyl record by a DJ using one and later two turntables, moving the needle back and forth between set portions of a vinyl record (backspinning or scratching). The words of the rapper (MC) play off and work through and around the beats of the

DJ, and 'hook' with the samples of other records (choruses, instrument breaks, etc.) which the DJ mixes in. Something of the skill involved is suggested by this description of a performance – using only two turntables – by one of the pioneers of the form, Grandmaster Flash, on an early track, 'The Adventures of Grandmaster Flash on the Wheels of Steel':

> It begins with 'you say one for the trouble', the opening phrase of Spoonie Gee's 'Monster Jam', broken down to 'you say' seven times, setting the tone for a record that uses the music and vocals of Queen's 'Another One Bites the Dust', the Sugar Hill Gang's '8th Wonder', and Chic's 'Good Times' as musical pawns that Flash manipulates at whim. He repeats 'Flash is bad' from Blondie's 'Rapture' three times, turning singer Deborah Harry's dispassion into total adoration. While playing 'Another One Bites the Dust', Flash places a record on the second turntable, then shoves the needle and the record against each other. The result is a grumbling, gruff imitation of the song's bassline. As the guitar feedback on 'Dust' builds, so does Flash's rumble, until we're grooving on 'Good Times'. Next, 'Freedom' explodes between the pauses in Chic's 'Good Times' bassline. His bass thumps, and then the Furious Five chant, 'Grandmaster cuts faster'. Bass. 'Grandmaster'. Bass. 'Cut'. Bass. 'Cuts . . . cuts . . . faster'. But the cold crusher comes at the end when, during '8th Wonder' Flash places a wheezing sound of needle on vinyl in the spaces separating a series of claps. (Nelson George, quoted in Rose 1994: 54)

Rap began in the South Bronx in New York City as part of hip-hop, 'an African-American and Afro-Caribbean youth culture composed of graffiti, breakdancing and rap music. From the outset, rap music has articulated the pleasures and problems of black urban life in contemporary America' (Rose 1994: 2). With the prominence and popularity of rap, the attention it receives in the media (though much of it adverse), and its commercial success, it is often treated as if it were an entirely new phenomenon. In fact, as David Toop argues, rap is 'a word that has been part of Afro-American vocabulary for a long time' (1984: 8): 'Rap's forebears stretch back through disco, street funk, radio DJs, Bo Diddley, the bebop singers, Cab Calloway, Pigmeat Markham, the tap dancers and comics, The Last Poets, Gil Scott-Heron, Muhammad Ali, acapella and doo-wop groups, ring games, skip-rope rhymes, prison and army songs, toasts, signifying and the dozens, all the way to the griots of Nigeria and Gambia' (1984: 19). Certainly POC's tribute to Dollar Brand (Abdullah Ibrahim) on the cover of *Our World*, and the contribution of Shaheen's father, jazz musician Issy Ariefdien, as both co-producer and musician on the first two albums suggest that they too perceive rap as part of a continuing black musical history.

Rap was from the start a form expressing urban identity and agency: 'North American blacks, Jamaicans, Puerto Ricans, and other Caribbean people with roots in other postcolonial contexts reshaped their cultural identities and expressions in a hostile, technologically sophisticated, multi-ethnic, urban terrain. Although city leaders and the popular press had literally and figuratively condemned the South Bronx neighbourhoods and their inhabitants, its youngest black and Hispanic residents answered back' (Rose 1994: 34). DJs such as Kool Herc would set up impromptu street performances with massive sound systems and beatboxes or ghetto-blasters, tapping illegal power from streetlights. The control and manipulation of visual and sound technology were at the centre of rap's social and aesthetic ontology from the start:

> At a time when cuts in school music programs drastically reduced access to traditional forms of instrumentation and composition, inner-city youths increasingly relied on recorded sound. Breakdancers used their bodies to mimic 'transformers' and other futuristic robots in symbolic street battles. Early Puerto Rican, Afro-Caribbean, and black American hip-hop artists transformed obsolete vocational skills from

> marginal occupations into the raw materials for creativity and resistance. (Rose 1994: 34–35)

The first commercial rap singles were 'Rapper's Delight' by the Sugar Hill Gang, and the rather less successful 'King Tim III (Personality Jock)' by The Fatback Band. Early rap bands included Grandmaster Flash and The Furious Five, Afrika Bambaataa and the Cosmic Force, The Tremendous Three, and The Funky Four Plus One More. From its fugitive beginnings, rap has become an international musical force – particularly following the (often ambiguous) publicity of so-called gangsta rappers of the 1980s (Ice T, NWA, Ice Cube and Too Short), the film projects of Spike Lee, the launch of an MTV rap channel (and locally OTV), and the more recent public debate around controversial white rapper Eminem (Marshall Mathers). Indeed, rap is fast becoming a global episteme.

* * *

> Rap is the Black man's CNN.
> *Chuck D, Public Enemy (Stapleton 1998: 222)*

> It's the way you talk, the way you walk . . . whatever you do is hip-hoppified.
> *Sparrow (Watkins 2000: 105)*

> It might be that to truly understand hip-hop you need a masters degree in sociology, a stint in the joint, and an intimate understanding of African rhythm.
> *George (1998: ix)*

There have been various critical and theoretical accounts of rap and hip-hop internationally, including those by Rose, Toop, and Schumacher, and two studies of POC produced locally, by Haupt (1995) and Watkins (2000). Of the broad conceptual approaches to rap, I find Rose's the most compelling,[3] particularly in her attempts to write from within and outside of the academy, and her insistence on a contextual reading of hip-hop as emerging from conditions of urban dislocation and economic disempowerment. Rose's emphasis on postindustrial contextualisation does not, however, entail a denial of rap's roots in Afrodiasporic performance practices. Instead, she insists that '[i]t is the tension between the cultural fractures produced by postindustrial oppression and the binding ties of black cultural expressivity that sets the critical frame for the development of hip hop' (1994: 21).

Several critics overemphasise either the pre-modern or post-modern aspects of rap: stressing exclusively its origins in (West) African performance traditions, or locating it almost entirely within the realm of postmodern play/pastiche (especially through its use of sampled sounds). Yet central to rap and hip-hop is their drawing together, in contexts of differentiated modernities and post-modernities, advanced technological and 'traditional' performance techniques into forms which claim, and accomplish, an identity of belonging. This traditional/technological conjunction is epitomised, for example, in rappers' dismissal of certain samplers and drum machines for sounding 'too white', and their recording 'into the red' to turn technology to new cultural expressivities. Rose rejects both pre- and postmodern readings of hip-hop, and wishes instead to show 'how hip hop's primary properties . . . simultaneously reflect and contest the social roles open to urban inner-city youths at the end of the twentieth century' (1994: 22).

Beadle has suggested that rap is 'to the black American urban youth more or less what punk was to its British white counterpart' (1993: 77). The analogy is a good one, particularly in view of the tendency in both forms to combine the social with the antisocial, the progressive with the reactionary, and the pleasurable with the political. There has been much media coverage of the destructive, violent, misogynist and racist aspects of rap music. Ronald Ferguson, a black Harvard academic at the university's John F. Kennedy School of Government, even believes that rap and hip-hop 'may be responsible for the sharp decline in examination results, especially the decline in reading and mathematic abilities' ('Hip Hop and Rap

Blamed' 2000). In reply, rappers emphasise the educative aspects of hip-hop culture, going so far, in the case of South African rapper Emile (himself an ex-school teacher), as to claim that it is more educative than formal schooling (Watkins 2000: 58). In response to rap's bad press – which many feel simply reflects broader racist perceptions of black culture – and drawing on perceptions such as Emile's above, some critics have overcompensated by presenting rap almost exclusively as social upliftment. Watkins, for example, defines the form (and his own intellectual project) in somewhat messianic terms:

> Informants emphasise the importance of being positive, and of structuring their identities by way of the relationship they have with their environment. Hip-hop builds the individual's strength within the collective crew. Identities are split between the individual and the crew, yet this boundary is blurred when the crew is mobilised, or mobilising. Since hip-hoppers organise themselves into crews, their expressions allude to a form of group identification nurtured by the promise of an empowered self. For them, the production and consumption of rap music is an overt political process which generates feelings and relationships which enable them to think positively, and behave competently in fields that are not musical. (2000: 60)

As a result, in what is otherwise a fascinating study, Watkins does not really move beyond what the hip-hoppers themselves claim they are doing into a critical interrogation of rap and rappers. A crucial part of such an interrogation should involve also those aspects of the form less amenable to critical recuperation. Watkins himself quotes some of the more flippant or confrontational statements of rappers, including Sparrow's memorable 'If I want to motherfuck I can motherfuck, if I want to shit I can shit' (2000: 63), but he does not tie the deliberately dangerous or pleasurable aspects of rap centrally to the form.[4]

The double-valency of the term 'bad' in hip-hop speak – pleasurable/cutting-edge and/or dangerous – points to the crucial duality at the heart of the culture and its lifestyle, which must be central to any critical engagement. The members of POC point to the ambiguous responses of family members to their music: a combination of pride at their achievements and discomfort that their chosen form is '*daai vloek musiek*' (that swearing music). When talking about how he got into hip-hop, Ready D emphasises the social/political affinities between black United States and South African contexts: 'Everything the people were speaking about, we could basically feel and understand it, because we share the same war stories, we share the same ghetto stories, because it all started out in the same poverty-stricken areas'. But he also refers to sheer musical groove: 'Man, I can't give a specific reason why we started, but one is . . . I mean everything we encountered as far as hip-hop goes was just, as James Brown would say, too damn funky!' (Magnette 1997). The project of rap is (also) in the jams and the play, in making the urban space funky and liveable. POC participate in voter education and literacy programmes, but they live the perils and pleasures of the Cape Flats, carrying handguns to protect themselves from gang violence while knowing 'how to rock a party', to rap 'to the rhythm of the bass' ('Kickin' Non-Stop'). Raoul, from the Cape Town crew Grave Diggers Productions, talks of hip-hop giving 'you something there . . . like gravity' (Watkins 2000: 29), but it is clear that gravity does not imply gravitas: part of rap's purpose is to disrupt, to ridicule, to overcome, with the power of its sonic assault; the reason is in the rhyme.

* * *

> Most of my heroes don't appear on stamps.
> *Public Enemy, 'Fight the Power'*

> I like doin' hip-hop because I'm from the Kaap.
> *POC, 'The Roof is on Fire'*

> Question: What do you want to be when you get older?
> Answer: Older!
> *Well-known joke from the Cape Flats (Friedman 1998)*

Hip-hop and rap are forms of urban location: graffiti 'tags' and slogans cover walls and trains; bass-heavy beats thump out of cars, minibuses and buildings; the distinctive style and clothing (constantly changing, but including oversized pants and jackets, overtly branded athletic wear, bandannas, baseball caps and heavy jewellery) are everywhere. In De Certeau's terms (1984), the 'place' of urban impoverishment and regulation becomes the 'space' of hip-hop movement and assertion; the official 'strategy' is countered by the mobile 'tactic' of style and performance.

While there were developments in other centres, rap in South Africa really began in Cape Town in the early 1980s. The centre was initially Club T-zers, later renamed The Base, at which the African Hip-Hop Alliance, based on 'black empowerment and mutual respect', was formed (Eyal 2000). Groups included The Ballastic Rockers (later to become POC), The Freaks, Chill Crush Crew, Organised Rhyme, Jam B, Cool Posse, AK 47, Sisters in Command, Cool Out Crew, TMD, MC Revolt, Sell Out Syndicate, The Supreme Breakers, The Break Xplosion, The Dream Team Breakers, The Pop Glide Breakers, and the Cape Town City Breakers. POC's Shaheen and Ready D were at the forefront of developments from the beginning, the latter having honed his DJing skills during a period in Liverpool, sponsored by a young white hip-hopper from Cape Town, DJ Aski, who had moved to the United Kingdom to avoid military conscription.

Rap and hip-hop were ambiguously placed in the South African political struggles of the 1980s. Rappers and breakdancers performed at political rallies, and Ready D and Shaheen, in particular, took part in several resistance actions, but hip-hop was also criticised for being politically 'irrelevant', particularly in its American influences and its emphasis on expensive brand names. However, hip-hop has a central and continuing role in claiming a rooted, yet modern, urban identity and belonging. Ironically, it may have greater purchase and currency for many in present circumstances than what are perceived to be the rather stale, or anachronistic, struggle narratives and roles of the past. In Watkins's suggestive phrase, rappers continue to be 'voices from behind the railway line' (2000: 48), speaking of the problems and pleasures of black urban life.

Hip-hop in South Africa is closely linked with the urban locale of the Cape Flats and its history of gangsterism. When explaining the origins of the group's name, Ready D says: '[W]e grew up in gang-infested areas, the area with a high degree of poverty going on . . . so the reason we choose Prophets of da City is to tell people man . . . it's easy to predict what's going to happen. If we get into this whole drug and gang bullshit that is going on' (Watkins 2000: 54). The band members themselves have a history of involvement in gang-related activities, and perceive POC and hip-hop as an escape route, as an alternative form of identification and commitment. 'All my friends were in gangs,' says Ready D. 'A lot of them are in prison for murder. Everyone expected me to go down that route. I can remember when people were stabbed for a pair of Ray Bans' (Rouse 1995). Even though the band is now based in Johannesburg for professional reasons, POC's social and imaginative location remains the Cape Flats.

Friedman links the emergence of gangsterism on the Cape Flats particularly with the context of apartheid's forced removals:

> Gangsterism, of course, was there before the removals, but it was influenced mainly by Chicago-style gangs, too busy taking pot shots at each other to take it out on the rest of the community. And relentless police action, during the 1940s in particular, kept the gangs under control.
>
> But the forced removals provided fertile gangster soil for a community forced to contend with cultural, economic and political dispossession. Gangsterism flourished alongside unemployment, alienation and anger. Today it is estimated that there are at least 80 000 gangsters in the Cape Flats area alone. (1998)

She quotes a 1996 study by Pinnock and Douglas-Hamilton in which they found that

> in communities stricken by poverty, racism, broken homes or drugs, there was an ever-present danger that emotions usually held in check by social pressure might be released. Among disadvantaged youth in particular, the search for 'respect' in the crossing to adulthood takes on larger-than-life proportions. Gangs provide glamour, status and a road to respect seemingly beyond reach through conventional behaviour. (Friedman 1998)

In this context, in which in one area safe passage for children to school is guaranteed by a temporary truce, agreed to by gangs and police, signalled by the blowing of a whistle, POC have involved themselves in several initiatives, including the African Hip Hop Alliance Support network, to offer young people a 'way out'. The form and its lifestyle become means of reclaiming identity, agency and location.

This reclaiming is most powerfully evident in the videos that accompany most rap songs. Often self-produced and funded, the videos generally follow a similar format, involving the rappers and their posses (the term 'homeboy' connoting the importance of belonging) within the 'hood. As Rose argues:

> Rappers' emphasis on posses and neighbourhoods has brought the ghetto back into the public consciousness. It satisfies poor young black people's profound need to have their territories acknowledged, recognized, and celebrated. These are the street corners and neighbourhoods that usually serve as lurid backdrops for street crimes on the nightly news. Few local people are given the opportunity to speak, and their points of view are always contained by expert testimony. In rap videos, young mostly black male residents speak for themselves and for the community, they speak when

> and how they wish about subjects of their own choosing. These local turf scenes are not isolated voices; they are voices from a variety of social margins that are in dialogue with one another. (1994: 11)

Although, as I have suggested, POC's primary imaginative and social location remains the Cape Flats, they increasingly claim, and speak for, a more generic black urban identity and location. A journalist offers this account of travelling through Soweto with the band:

> Shaheen points to where POC did their most recent video. The site is a playing field littered with debris. Near to the swings, which no longer have the chains and seats dangling from the crossbar, a rubbish-filled skip smoulders. There are no kids playing there. The equipment looks like extinct dinosaurs, just fossilised remains of former magnificence. Lance pulls up at a heavily fortified general store. [There is a] piece Gogga [POC's own graphic/spray-can artist] did for the elections, with that slogan 'Never Again' sprawling across the wall. Shaheen and Ramone climb inside the barbed wire that the proprietor of the shop has proudly erected to safeguard this masterpiece.
>
> 'Hey Stephen, listen', Lance calls over. 'The kids over there . . .', he adds gesturing across the road. A group of young children inside the perimeter of the house opposite are shrieking and wailing. They have spotted Shaheen and Ramone posing for pictures and they are quoting Mandela and singing Prophets lyrics. 'Never again, never again', they squeal, running away as the cameras turned on them. (Worthy 1994: 49)

* * *

Would you like me to sing you a lullaby?
I want a rap song.
POC, 'Bass Drive'

> Who's in the house?
> Prophets of the City getting busy
> Are you with me?
> *POC, 'Intro – Prophets Getting Busy'*

> I think POC contributed somehow in exposing hip-hop to a large part of the country who didn't know that hip-hop existed . . . 'cause we performed in places where there was no electricity and dust roads and you had to use four or five extension cables to get electricity, and we performed in places where people didn't know you can use a turntable as an instrument and there was music where there wasn't actually instruments, and the type of dancing . . . .
> *Shaheen (Watkins 2000: 55)*

The process by which I got hold of the POC albums says much about the ambiguities, contradictions and possibilities of the form itself. I could find nothing whatsoever in Durban, where I was living at the time, whether from mainstream outlets (such as Musica and Look & Listen) or from independent or informal vendors. I finally found a copy of *Age of Truth* in East London, and had to mail-order *Ghetto Code* from the African Music Store in Cape Town. Eventually I contacted POC's record company, Ghetto Ruff, and was greeted with real warmth and kindness by Delphine Klassen and Lance Stehr (POC's manager). I was informed that even they only had vinyl copies of *Our World* and *Boom Style*, and an album of 12-inch remixes off *Phunk Phlow*, but offered them all to me at no charge, together with a stack of press clippings. It seems the only remaining copy of *Phunk Phlow* at Ghetto Ruff has been lent to a film company making a documentary on POC – an act as risky as it is generous, which seems aptly to characterise POC and crew.

From the first beat of their debut album, POC signalled that theirs was a local interpretation of hip-hop, offering 'rich portrayals of locally embedded and globally connected performance practices' (Erlmann 1996: 12). The songs are strongly influenced by South

African musical genres, with rap weaving across and through the instrumentation. In comparison to the later material, which is heavier, more aggressive and dissonant, the production is more melodic and bass-lite. The handwritten sleeve notes say: 'The music on this rap album is influenced by the music and people we grew up with. We chose to do this album different from your average rap LP so that our people can relate to it easily (goema, kwela, jazz, disco, lang arm and POC music, Abdullah Ibrahim [Dollar Brand])'. This sentiment is also echoed in the song 'Musical Madness' from the second album, which talks explicitly of using more familiar genres to draw audiences into rap and hip-hop.

The sleeve notes also offer a topography of Cape Town – simultaneously naming and claiming the place in a linguistically transitive act (analogous to that made by Ronnie Govender as discussed in Chapter 5): 'Lavis . . . Black Heath . . . Hanover Park . . . Parkwood . . . Elsie's River . . . Ravensmead . . . Woodstock en die Salts . . . Bonitas . . . Mitchell's Plain . . . Bonta's'. This naming finds musical accompaniment in the forms mentioned above. In the song 'I Remember District Six' from their album *Ghetto Code*, POC explicitly link their sound and performance with a sense of placement and displacement, combining oral testimony, melodic jazz, and the rapper's own voice of remembrance:

> I remember the days in District Six
> The laughter of adults and little kids
> Hanover Street and the markets with fish
> Goema music was always the heartbeat
> I remember the days of District Six
> The sound of the snoekhorn and the ouens used to
> Break with a lekker song.

As Rose argues, rappers 'tell long, involved, and sometimes abstract stories with catchy and memorable phrases and beats that lend themselves to black sound bite packaging, storing critical narratives in fast-paced electrified rhythms' (1994: 3). A crucial part of this narrativisation involves naming, not only of place, but of person(a). As I indicated at the beginning of this chapter, the POC members have hip-hop names, which testify to their status and prowess (DSA means 'Dominator of Sound All Around'; 'DJ X-Plode' is the one who 'wrecks the decks'). It is particularly in performance that this aspect of hip-hop is evident, as rappers claim and enact – in a manner that stresses the affinities between rap and praise poetry or 'boasting' – their ability and identity. This is often through aggressive metaphors and barbed 'disses' (critical, insulting or 'disrespectful' comments). Even on the first album, the lyrics of which tend towards the ameliorative, stressing social upliftment and an end to crime and violence, the song 'Murder on Stage' presents the MC's superior lyrical ability as the literal annihilation of opposition:

> I'm a definite threat to you and your posse
> You wanna be bossy
> Showing off with your gold that's glossy
> But that's basically all you can show
> Put you on the stage, can you flow? No no
> But then comes DSA and Ready D
> You wanna step to us, just let us be
> Cause I'm a poltergeist on the rise
> I'll cut you down to size.
> . . .
> I'm the assassin with a rhyming passion
> Cruisin' along, crashin' and bashin'
> . . .
> So I strangle, you can't handle
> You say you burn, but I blow you like a candle
> . . .
> Murder, murder on stage.

It is clear that the band sees the 'controlled' violence of hip-hop performance as an alternative to the destructiveness of gangsterism and drug use, but the aggressive competitiveness they enact is a crucial aspect of hip-hop's attraction for urban youth, and one that criticism must acknowledge. At the centre of the performance space, lyrically and visually, is the 'mic', and sound amplification becomes for rappers 'a life-giving source' (Rose 1994: 22): they claim and patrol the stage, flaunting their style and movement, displaying their mastery of sound and technology.

For POC, hip-hop – which they call 'the culture' – is crucially linked with Black Consciousness and the process of self-affirmation. Ready D says of POC's mission:

> The basic principle is just to be real to yourself, trying to respect yourself and the culture. That is the basic principle we operate on. It's a hip-hop thing, we think of hip-hop before we do anything else. Because we don't see ourselves as doing hip-hop, we see ourselves as hip-hop because we live this on a day-to-day basis. (Watkins 2000: 55)

For Ready D and other band members this involves reading people such as Steve Biko, Marcus Garvey, Malcom X and others, as well as a proper knowledge of, and respect for, black cultural traditions. The songs constantly articulate this reclamation of blackness: 'Black man raise your fist, say what you say' ('Power 2 da People'); 'I don't have blue eyes, I don't have blonde hair/ I'm black to the bone' ('Remember Where You Came From'); or 'Fuck "Die Stem" it's the white man's anthem' ('African Very African'). Largely because of their directly political position, POC have battled over the artistic control and distribution of their work. The band members claim that their first two albums involved a great deal of compromise with regard to the way in which they represented themselves because conditions were very oppressive, and they themselves were inexperienced in dealing with the recording industry (Haupt 1995: 47). Despite their apparent moderation, however, 'Roots' and 'Ons Stem' from the first and second albums respectively were banned.

With the release of *Age of Truth* in October 1993, however, the band took increasing responsibility for the material and greater advantage of the less restrictive political context. Whereas even the word 'SHIT' was censored to 'S–T' on the sleeve notes of the first album, *Age of Truth* includes lines such as 'Fuck Mangope even if we record here', which led to their DAT tapes being confiscated by Bophuthatswana police and Tusk music having its lawyers (literally) 'counting the fucks'. The album specifically attacked the National Party and the apartheid security establishment, which was still very much in evidence, and most of the tracks were either banned or prohibited from being played on SABC television or radio.[5] After 1994, Lance Stehr approached the SABC to get some airtime for the album and video, but was told that the SABC no longer bans tracks, it simply does not play them (Haupt 1995: 67 fn.). After the hard-hitting bass and dissonance of *Phunk Phlow*, POC feel that their latest album *Ghetto Code* is far more accessible. Despite Ready D's sense that '[t]he music is not as harsh as it used to be on previous albums' (Feldman 1997), and Shaheen's claim that 'This record is something for South African audiences who supported us. We are finally doing what you wanted us to do' (Feldman 1997), there was and still is little radio or television exposure.

* * *

My gesig is so swart soos die nag
En jy staan en lag
Met jou mag het jy ons mense verkrag
Jy het vergeet van die dag van gebod
My wapen is my mond
En dit sal ontplof soos 'n bom.[6]
POC, 'Ons Stem'

This is a sampling sport.
Public Enemy, 'Caught, Can we Get a Witness'

Like most rappers, POC pay careful attention to the lyrical form of their songs. Ready D talks of the importance of being able 'to rap in different styles . . . get the different styles of lyrics . . . to be able to do like similes, metaphors . . . to . . . throw it around and so on' (Watkins 2000: 62); and Shaheen says: 'As far as the media and that hype is concerned it means absolutely nothing. I find more joy if somebody comes to me and says that, "the line you used in such and such a song where you used alliteration into a metaphor into a simile into a pun, like in two lines, that was kwaai"' (Watkins 2000: 108). More than with any other oral form, perhaps, rap must be heard: it is crucially rhythm, rhyme and verbal inflection – and the syncopation of these with sound and beat. Rhythm and rhyme in the lyrics may depend on verbal 'playing' with syllabic length and stress to create complex, pleasing or disturbing patterns and emphases. A 'literary' scanning of a few lines from 'Boomstyle' for rhythm and rhyme would be as follows:

˘ / ˘ ˘ / ˘ ˘ / ˘ ˘ / ˘ / ˘
a b c b b
They blew me away that is only what they say to build up

˘ / ˘ ˘ / ˘ / ˘ / ˘ / ˘
c a c (a?) c
Their egos, it was proven at many shows who flow and

/ ˘ ˘ ˘ / ˘ / ˘ /
c (c?) c c
Glow and have the power to overthrow

˘ / ˘ / ˘ ˘ / ˘ ˘ / ˘ / ˘
d d b c b e
And never get played like a domino game. I kick the

/ ˘ / / ˘ / ˘ ˘ / ˘ / ˘
d e d b e e b
Message and still entertain, with a mission I came to

/ / ˘ / ˘
d b b
Explain the aim, I'm

/ ˘ ˘ ˘ / ˘ ˘ /
b b b
Trained not to be lame on the brain . . .

Rhythm and rhyme are used particularly effectively by POC in destabilising official discourses. In the song 'Ons Stem', which opens with a brief sample from 'Die Stem', rhyme satirically undermines the former apartheid national anthem:

> Eendrag maak mag, ek wil lag
> want 'n hele ras, ongeag van geslag
> wag vir vryheid.[7]

This song was banned, yet continued to be performed – a contradiction at the centre of performance genres such as rap in which 'resistive transcripts are articulated and acted out in both hidden and public domains, making them highly visible, yet difficult to contain and confine' (Rose 1994: 101).

Drawing on the work of Arthur Jafa, Rose argues that hip-hop form centres on three concepts – flow, layering, and ruptures in line: 'In hip hop, visual, physical, musical, and lyrical lines are set in motion, broken abruptly with sharp angular breaks, yet they sustain motion and energy through fluidity and flow' (Rose 1994: 38).[8] As she points out, rappers speak constantly in their lyrics about 'flow' (or 'phlow'), 'referring to an ability to move easily and powerfully through complex lyrics as well as the flow of the music':

> The flow and motion of the initial bass or drum line in rap music is abruptly ruptured by scratching (a process that highlights as it breaks the flow of the base rhythm), or the rhythmic flow is interrupted by other musical passages.

> Rappers stutter and alternatively race through passages, always moving within the beat or in response to it, often using the music as a partner in rhyme. These verbal moves highlight lyrical flow and points of rupture. Rappers layer meaning by using the same word to signify a variety of actions and objects; they call out to the DJ to 'lay down a beat', which is expected to be interrupted, ruptured. DJs layer sounds literally one on top of each other, creating a dialogue between sampled sounds and words. (1994: 39)

A good example of this formal principle is in the POC song 'Understand Where I'm Coming From' on the album *Age of Truth*. The song opens with a musical sample, ruptured by scratching and then with Mzwakhe Mbuli's voice layered over saying 'Listen to the voices', which flows into the choral refrain 'Hlanganani'. Rupture is introduced as the Latin '*Dulce et decorum est pro patria mori*' ('It is sweet and fitting to die for one's country') is rapped, though the lyrics flow from the Latin through the rhyme ('Mori . . . sorry . . . story . . . for me'): 'I'm sorry that story's not for me'. Rupture is introduced again about four lines later as the rhythm and bassline change with the interjection: 'and it's not a funny sight, 'cause money's tight . . .'. Rose argues that this formal model is functional within rap's negotiation of urban space and identity:

> Interpreting these concepts theoretically, one can argue that they create and sustain rhythmic motion, continuity, and circularity via flow; accumulate, reinforce, and embellish this continuity through layering; and manage threats to these narratives by building in ruptures that highlight the continuity as they momentarily challenge it. These effects at the level of style and aesthetics suggest affirmative ways in which profound social dislocation and rupture can be managed and perhaps contested in the cultural arena. Let us imagine these hip hop principles as a blueprint for social resistance and affirmation: create sustaining narratives, accumulate them,

layer them, embellish and transform them. However, be also prepared for rupture, find pleasure in it, *plan on* social rupture. When these ruptures occur, use them in creative ways that will prepare you for a future in which survival will demand a sudden shift in ground tactics. (1994: 39)

Central to rap's formal and social articulation is the use of sampled sounds. Whereas samplers were originally intended to save time in the recording process, rappers have made them into musical instruments, reconceptualising the technology within their own aesthetic paradigms. POC often use samples to undermine colonial or apartheid discourses. 'Blast from da Past', a 53-second track from *Age of Truth* is constructed entirely from samples, aggressively countering racist historiography with voices of black assertion and 'noise':

'More than three hundred years ago . . .' [Voice of officialdom]
'The revolution . . .' [Black American rapper/politician]
'Africa shall know no peace until we in the south are free' [Mzwakhe Mbuli]
'Time is running out' [distorted]
'Daar kom die Alibama' [sung]
'Ons Suid-Afrika' [x3], 'Jan van Riebeeck' [Afrikaans male voice]
'FUCK OFF' [POC]
'A commander whose name was Jan van Riebeeck' [Afrikaans male voice]
'FUCK OFF' [POC] . . . 'Jan' . . . 'FUCK OFF' . . . 'Jan' . . . 'FUCK OFF' . . . 'Jan van Riebeeck' . . . 'FUCK OFF'
'The revolution' [Black American rapper/politician]
Bassline
'Jan van Riebeeck' . . . 'FUCK OFF'
'Jan van Riebeeck' . . . 'FUCK OFF'
'Jan van Riebeeck' . . . 'FUCK OFF'

'Ons Suid Afrika' . . . 'FUCK OFF'
'When the Hottentot men shoot at us with their bows and arrows, they will not harm us.' [Afrikaans male voice]
'Time is running out' [x3]
'FUCK OFF' [POC].

It is certainly possible to read such use of samples in postmodern ways as 'unsettl[ing] the hegemonic practice of controlling polysemy or play in the signification process which, ultimately, violently suppresses any attempts by those on the margins to articulate difference' (Haupt 1995: 56). However, a more productive and challenging contention is, as certain critics have suggested, to link rap's use of samples to the history of black performative practice, which Gates refers to as 'Signifyin(g)', 'turn[ing] on the play and chain of signifiers' (1987: 238), in which 'texts seem concerned to address their antecedents' (1988: 51). Indeed, it is difficult to distinguish conceptually between the use of a 'sample' in a rap song, and the 'borrowing' of praises in (for example) Zulu *izibongo*. Like many other hip-hop performers, POC perceive the sampling controversy in racial terms. Of their local albums only *Age of Truth* has an (incomplete) list of sample credits (though their United Kingdom release *Universal Souljaz* faced lengthy sample clearance delays), and Ready D says:

> But now you've got some record companies that's setting up some ridiculous publishing shit, you know, where . . . you've got to pay thousands of rands just to use a sample. And, I mean, hip hop is basically about fusing all type of stuff; scratching, you know, mixing . . . . So you get this white motherfucker doing all sorts of ridiculous shit and at the end of the day saying it's business, you know. And I mean, fuck that. Somebody want to sample our record it's fine by *me*. (Haupt 1995: 39)

Such an (inter)textual model offers radical challenges to Western/ capitalist notions of rights, ownership and property, and rappers and their record companies are constantly embroiled in legal disputes over copyright. As Schumacher (drawing on Frith) argues:

> '[C]opyright law defines music in terms of nineteenth-century Western conventions and is not well suited to the protection of African-American musicians' improvisational art.' The formal practices of Signifyin(g) in rap music defy traditional definitions of authorship because they are ultimately premised on referencing the other and by explicitly relying on previous utterances. (1995: 265)

He argues instead that approaches to rap need, as I suggested at the outset, to allow the form its own playfulness, irreverence and difficulty. He suggests that the 'Carnival' offers a more appropriate conceptual model than that of the individual creative artiste/author:

> Collins and Skover . . . present a 'cultural' analysis of free expression which they call 'pissing in the snow'. They suggest that actual speech practices (not idealised ones from legal theory) assume a Carnivalesque quality in that they tend not to abide by existing rules or laws. In the Carnival of popular culture, speech is directed more by the demands of listeners than by a fear of infringement:
>
> > The 'anarchistic' quality of the Carnival is fundamentally at odds with the notion of a government of laws. The very character of the Carnival is to push all boundaries, including the fixed lines of the law . . . (Schumacher 1995: 268)

Hence, like Ready D above, Schumacher advocates 'the freedom of unauthorized sampling, much in the spirit of the Carnival which respects no boundaries' (1995: 268–69).

The Carnival is fundamentally about pleasure – an aspect of rap that is particularly evident in its thumping bass and energetic dance. Curiously, especially in a thesis produced by a music student,

Watkins says that 'space and time' mean that he has had to leave various issues including 'musical analysis' and 'technology and rap' to 'be explored in further studies' (2000: 21). Certain of POC's songs have few political or social referents, in fact some have no lyrics at all, simply grooving on the scratching wizardry and rhythm of Ready D, and emphasising, on stage, extremely agile dance movement in an 'emotional performative sound event' (Negus 1998: 371). An understanding of rap music requires an alertness to rhythm, sound, noise and timbre rather than melodic sequence; it is first and foremost a (per)cussive form. DJs will sample beats from extremely obscure soul records to achieve exactly the sound they want, and will often record across more than one channel to manipulate noise to their satisfaction. Rose points out that since all rap artists are heavily confined and policed, even apparently 'apolitical' rap is heavily politicised (1994: 124), and she argues that displays of black pleasure and sexuality ('shakin' your thang') are often ideologically directed. POC emphasise bass rhythm within the sonic and performative space. The song 'Bass Drive' not only creates its own powerful rhythm but, as Haupt suggests, 'signifies' in its lyrics on the nature of bass (1995: 47): 'So don't waste time when u hear the bassline goes in time with the rhyme'. The bassline, which moves the dancers on the floor, becomes both metaphor for and actualisation of POC's force: 'POC is pumping bassdrive'. And an appreciation of bass defines the communal identity: 'We drop bass on the dance floor and leave it full of potholes/the only ones who survive are the ones who got soul'.

* * *

Step up if you don't know what DSA means
Or X-Plode's many tricks and when he picks a mix
More accurate than 1026
And when he kicks ballistics
I drop linguistics on this mix
So stay back 'cause I'm a maniac

> Time to pay back the ones who say that
> The prophets cannot really drop it
> *POC, 'Hard Time on Stage'*

A key aspect of performance and the articulation of identity is language. POC exhibit a great deal of reflexivity about language, being able to shift codes and registers on stage in relation to different audiences. Their most recent album *Ghetto Code* takes up the question of linguistic identity explicitly: '. . . so I think we're at a stage where we're trying to create our own style and our own identity. A lot of us are trying by first, to incorporate the language that we're speaking and we call it ghetto code, the type of code you speak where people don't understand you' (Shaheen, quoted in Watkins 2000: 55). There are two crucial aspects to POC's use of language. The first, evident in their decision to change their name in 1993 from Prophets of *the* City to Prophets of *da* City links with notions of a globalised black English, central to hip-hop but not restricted to it. The second relates to POC's use of linguistic codes or languages, including Afrikaans, which tie them more closely to notions of ethnic specificity. These two aspects – like so much in hip-hop and popular culture generally – are in both productive and problematic relationship.

The notion of a globalised black English is reflected in choices of vocabulary, phonology and orthography, through which POC and other rap bands wish to stress their connectedness – in the spirit of Black Consciousness – with disenfranchised people of African origin around the globe. (This language is clearly connected with that of fashion or style that has equivalent global valencies.) Spellings are altered ('phat' for 'fat', 'phlow' for 'flow', '4' for 'for', 'u' for 'you'); a vocabulary often impenetrable to others is adopted ('dope'– 'good', 'kicks' – 'shoes'); and apparently eccentric syntax and pronunciation are used. This language becomes a means of creating, sustaining and defending community, as well as a source of pleasure – what Rose refers to as '[d]eveloping a style nobody can deal with' (1994: 61).

However, in the same way that POC signal musically that they offer a localised (indigenised?) version of hip-hop, their use of language is also firmly rooted in South Africa, and specifically the Cape Flats. Shaheen, for example, says:

> We want to be street, you know? When we do interviews and shit like that and we speak gamtaal, or whatever, that shit's on purpose so the kid at home can say, 'Fuck, they're speaking my language,' you know? They're representing, you know, what comes out of the township and shit. So if some middle-class motherfucker comes, 'Oe God, skollietaal.' The shit's not *for* them, you know what I mean. I don't care if some white-ass dude at home thinks, 'Oh shit, look at this . . . uncultured', you know. I want some kid from the ghetto to think, 'Naa, we can relate to that.' (Haupt 1995: 65)

The strength of this is the music's rootedness in community, and POC's following in the Cape Flats is well established. Their use of local dialect, in this case of Afrikaans, is well illustrated in 'Dallah Flet 2':

> My broertjie kry 'n skoot dwars deur sy kop
> Want daar was 'n gang fight op onse blok.
> Die fight het gekom deur 'n gestryery oor dop en 'n stop
> All of a sudden gryp iemand 'n stok
> 'n Borrel word gebriek, 'n jong word gestiek,
> Sonder dat hy wiet is 'n nogge een geskiet . . . .[9]

The song is extremely effective in using 'ghetto code' to evoke the violence and social disorder of Cape Flats gangsterism, but it also risks reaffirming the process of ghettoisation. POC are aware of the dangers of being labelled as a 'Coloured' band. After an interview with *The Face* magazine in the United Kingdom, Ready D was concerned that so much was made of the 'Coloured' issue: 'I don't see myself as coloured, number one . . . and there is still no respect in South Africa for the so-called coloured population. Calling someone coloured is a total form of disrespect whether it comes from a black or a white man'. He recounts how, as a boy, he had to go through the indignity of the pencil test: 'They tried to stand a [pencil] in your hair and if it fell then you were classified as European and if it stuck you were coloured' (Rouse 1995). The band was similarly unhappy about a radio interview with Mark Gillman, at that time on Radio Good Hope, because of Gillman's constant attempts to portray them as 'gam'. Shaheen insists that their use of dialect on tracks such as 'Dallah Flet' has national appeal and represents an attempt to dissociate it from 'Coloured' identity, and that, with the inclusion of Ishmael and Danisa into the group, and their rapping in African languages, they are trying to steer away from being labelled 'gam' or 'Coloured' and so falling under Afrikaner Nationalist conceptions of ethnicity and racial identity (Haupt 1995: 66). The ambiguities of POC's position in this regard – simultaneously offering local affirmation/identification and exclusion/ethnicity – reflect broader uncertainties about difference and belonging. These are acute in South Africa in the post-apartheid context, but endemic to all postcolonial or 'multicultural' societies.

* * *

> I would like to thank: Lord God Almighty Allah for bringing us as far as we got and I pray that Allah may guide us as a people to unity and let peace prevail within us and on earth.
> *Ready D's 'Shout Out' on* Age of Truth

POC's name has deliberately religious connotations. Ready D says it refers to 'being witness and paying respect to all the great people and prophets . . . from Jesus to Moses, all the way to the prophet Mohammed. It's very social, very political and very spiritual' (Watkins 2000: 54). The album *Our World* is dedicated, amongst others, to 'All the Imams, Priests, Organisations and The Public who are fighting social diseases', and the sleeve notes to *Ghetto Code* contain further thanks to Allah. But often 'Allah' seems to be a shifting signifier for 'God' in a more pluralist sense, for Ishmael's shout out on the *Age of Truth* album reads, 'I would like to thank God and his son Jesus', and apparently does not contradict Ready D's claiming Islamic blessing for the band. Islam has been one of the strongest forces critiquing the hegemony of the West in localised or global politics, and has been central to the Black Consciousness organisations that have shaped the growth of hip-hop in the United States, particularly the Nation of Islam and Afrika Bambaataa's Zulu Nation. In South Africa and the Cape Flats specifically, Islam is closely bound up both with racial politics and the context of gangsterism. Perhaps because of the complexities of the issue, the danger of being misconstrued, and their own very genuine concern for tolerance (of which their shifting signification of God/Allah may be symptomatic) POC's religious identification is largely restricted to the sleeve notes.[10]

* * *

> Ek praat nou van 'n meit . . .[11]
> *POC, 'Dallah Flet 2'*

Rap's most resistant strain, and one frequently discussed in the media, is its gender politics. At least in part because of its alliance with the black nationalist discourses of Islam, and despite the emergence of women rappers such as Queen Latifa, Sister Souljah, Salt 'n Pepa, Lil' Kim or Missy Elliot, hip-hop 'follows in the steps of sixties black militancy by positioning black women who do not conform to the ideals of the patriarchal family structure as ungrateful wives or gold-digging lovers' (Decker 1993: 68). POC are in public support of gender equality, and Ready D himself has spoken about the importance of women being equals in hip-hop – though with some degree of confusion and apparently complete sublimation of the problems of Islam in this regard:

> You know especially growing up in a Western society . . . It teaches you that the man is the provider. He is much stronger and all this bullshit . . . so I think in the female subconscious that holds for the majority of females. Then you get the strong women that comes around and says, to hell with this . . . you know . . . if you're a man I'm able to get into your territory and still do damage in your scene . . . and that's the attitude that we like to encourage. We want to tell them that if you have a problem with whoever tell them this is a lot of bullshit . . . and come up with better skills and show them a thing or two. I'm not threatened by women participating. I think with females participating it will get the culture motivated much more. (Watkins 2000: 136)

Their lyrics occasionally suggest otherwise, though. 'Dallah Flet 2' addresses a 'Coloured' woman with the apartheid appellation of 'meit',[12] and rejects claims of paternity with an aggressively racist and sexist diatribe:

> Of soek jy 'n pa vir jou laaitie
> Jy hou nou haaitie taaitie
> But daai issie alright nie
> Wat ek mean om to sê
> Jy was gewillig om to lê
> But now you wanna give me a scare
> 'Cause the baby is there
> I may be 'n derra, 'n pa
> Maar Ramone was ook daar
> Moenie kla nie, ek issie vaakie
> Nege maande gelede was ek nie eers innie Kaapie
> Dis 'n haatie, jy't nie 'n saak nie
> Hou jou mond, moenie eers praat nie
> Want jy kan niks maakie
> Genoeg van daai
> Ek praat nou van 'n meit

> . . .
> Jy's stuck up, jy's fucked up en wat
> Wat dink jy jy is wit met jou swart gat . . .[13]

Such sentiments are difficult to deal with, and rap's misogyny (and racism) has provided ample ammunition to its detractors. Nelson George is correct, though, in claiming of hip-hop in the United States that it should not be held to sole account for more widespread social prejudices: 'Despite the "dangerous" edge of so much hip hop culture, all of its disturbing themes are rooted in this country's dysfunctional values. Anti-Semitism, racism, violence, and sexism are hardly unique to rap stars but are the most sinister aspects of the national character' (George 1998: xiii). Rose, while herself extremely critical of sexism within rap, concurs: 'Rap's contradictory articulations are not signs of absent intellectual clarity; they are a common feature of community and popular cultural dialogues that always offer more than one cultural, social, or political viewpoint. These unusually abundant polyvocal conversations seem irrational when they are severed from the social contexts where everyday struggles over resources, pleasure, and meanings take place' (1994: 2). Indeed, she goes further, stressing that its contradictions and conservatisms are often what give hip-hop popular attraction and should not simply be suppressed by 'progressive' political agendas:

> [T]hese contradictions [are] *central* to hip hop and to popular cultural articulations in general. Hip hop's liberatory, visionary, and politically progressive elements are deeply linked to those regressive elements that Willis believes 'sell the tradition short'. This aspect of hip hop's contradictions is not unique to postmodernity, it is a central aspect of popular expression and popular thought. In other words, cultural forms contain cultural ideas and ways of thinking that are already part of social life. In fact, it is these contradictions that make the culture coherent and relevant to the society in which it operates. It is the contradictory nature of

> pleasure and social resistance in the popular realm that must be confronted, theorized, and understood, instead of erasing it or rigidly rejecting those practices that ruin our quest for untainted politically progressive cultural expressions. (Rose 1994: 24)

* * *

> Rap music is one of the most heavily traded popular commodities in the market, yet it still defies total corporate control over the music, its local use and incorporation at the level of stable or exposed meanings.
>
> *Rose (1994: 41)*

> [T]he combi, which had been jumping about like a bucking bronco for an hour, finally loses power. There's a problem with the fuel pump.
>
> *Account of POC on the way to a gig (Worthy 1994: 46)*

There are many metaphors we could use in writing about hip-hop in South Africa. Dror Eyal describes what he perceives to be hip-hop's decline in the face of kwaito in terms of a subway tunnel: 'Hip-Hop has gone back underground to its roots, back to the deep bass rumble at the bottom of a graffiti-covered tunnel' (2000: 4). Watkins uses the train line as his central metaphor for discussing hip-hop in Cape Town, a metaphor that implies and maintains social movement and division. He quotes one Cape Town hip-hopper who comments, somewhat caustically, that although POC travel by car, their videos maintain the centrality of the train as a symbol for the traversing of urban space (Watkins 2000: 31). And yet, POC's actual mode of transport is richly suggestive. Articles on the band refer constantly to their vehicle's breaking down as they traverse major and minor roads taking their music to communities throughout the country. Perhaps most emblematic of their achievements in South Africa, despite – or because of – a lack of institutional recognition is their inadvertently – and spectacularly – topping the bill at the 2000 Splashy Fen music festival because by the time they arrived after yet another breakdown the only slot left was that of the headline band.

* * *

When Douglas Livingstone died, a letter of obituary appeared in *The Daily News* that mourned his passing in terms that resonate with the question with which this book began: 'If this is your land, where are your stories?':

> The poems which he set in Durban have defined for many readers a sense of place – the harbour, the old whaling station, the fishermen, the tall blocks of flats on the beachfront and esplanade, the expanses of beach and surf stretching north and south . . . Douglas Livingstone often evoked the loneliness of urban experience in his poems. Durban seems a lonelier place for his passing. (Gray 1996)

Like Livingstone's poems, or Bushman storytelling and rock painting, which express, enact and accomplish a sense of belonging, rap, hip-hop and spray-can art claim the urban space, enable its use and mediate its meanings: the place is a name is a song is movement is style is a story is a map is despair is hope.

Notes

Introduction

1. Chamberlin (2003) has used this question as the title for a book in which he offers a wide-ranging discussion of issues of narrative, community and identity.
2. I am aware of the extensive debate about the terms 'Bushman' and 'San', and the problems of both terms. When referring to specific societies, I use the term employed by members of that society for self-reference (!Kung, /Xam, etc.). Where I refer to such people more broadly, I use the term 'Bushman' or 'Bushmen'. I use the term 'Aboriginal' (upper case) to refer to the indigenous peoples of Australia, and 'aboriginal' (lower case) to refer to 'first peoples' generally, that is, to those who have, as far as the evidence suggests, been in their areas 'from the beginning' (*ab origine*). There is extensive debate worldwide at present around the terms 'aboriginal' and 'indigenous', which space does not allow me to engage with here. Some of the arguments and counter-arguments are detailed in De Villiers (1997); see also Gordon (1992).

Chapter 1: Stories of Land, Land of Stories

1. The question of whether the term 'nation' may legitimately be used for such groupings is a complex one that is too lengthy to be dealt with here. As many of the societies themselves use this term in making their claims, I have simply kept to their usage.
2. The terms are drawn from Jameson (1988).
3. I am indebted to Chamberlin (1998 and 2001) for my account of this court case.
4. This seminar paper was published, in somewhat different form, in 2002. In this chapter I quote the earlier version.
5. See, for example, Guenther (1989), Hewitt (1986) and Brown (1998).

6. These postmodern social movements range from 'new age' spiritualities and environmental pantheism, to a variety of urban counter- or sub-cultures which involve tattooing, body-piercing and scarification.
7. Since much of //Kabbo's time with Bleek and Lloyd was spent in telling stories, there is probably no better assertion of the distinction between oral literature as social activity and oral literature as the subject of academic study, especially that produced in artificial contexts of transcription and translation.
8. The parentheses and other unusual punctuation marks in the English versions of the /Xam texts quoted here reflect Bleek and Lloyd's efforts to indicate uncertainties or areas of unintelligibility in the transcription and translation process.
9. In the court case DelgamUukw vs. the Queen, the state was at pains to argue that the 'acculturation' of the Gitksan and Wet'suwet'en (their use of wills and hunting/fishing permits was claimed as evidence for this) invalidated their claims to 'aboriginal' rights.
10. Liebenberg says:

    > In the narrowest sense of the word 'spoor' simply means 'footprint', but in tracking it has a much wider meaning, including all signs found on the ground or indicated by disturbed vegetation. Tracking also involves signs such as scent, urine and faeces, saliva, pellets, feeding signs, vocal and other auditory signs, visual signs, incidental signs, circumstantial signs, blood spoor, skeletal signs, paths, homes and shelters. Leaves and twigs rolling in the wind, long grass sweeping the ground or dislodged stones rolling down a steep slope leave their distinctive spoor. Markings left by implements, weapons or objects may indicate the activities of the persons who used them, and vehicles also leave tracks. (1990: 111)

11. The film, *The Great Dance*, by Craig and Damon Foster, explores the processes of reading spoor and the training required.
12. Liebenberg's argument in this respect is supported by the fact that – in Kalahari Bushman societies – the custom of sharing meat means that very successful hunters might refrain from hunting too often so as not to provoke jealousy or a sense of inequality (1990: 55).
13. At a conference that I attended in 1994, entitled 'Texts and Images of People, Politics and Power: Representing the Bushman People of South Africa' (Rock Art Research Unit, University of the Witwatersrand and the Johannesburg Art Gallery), representatives of the various Bushman

communities present spoke forcefully of the need for academic research to lead to material improvements in their lives, specifically the sinking of boreholes and the building of roads and bridges.

14. Since my initial interview in 1999, I have maintained contact with André Truter. Following the project's initial success, and because of his own developing business interests, Truter handed over management of the project to the community organisation Farm Watch. As a result of what appear to have been communication problems between management and the trackers, a period of uncertainty and unhappiness on all sides ensued. The project is now under Truter's coordination again, and is working well, though in a slightly different way. Under the new arrangement the trackers themselves are employed directly by farmers, and most choose to remain in employment for a period of two years or so, following which they return to their community with capital that they can use to purchase livestock and/or farming materials or establish some form of livelihood.
15. In Australia Chatwin's biographer, Nicholas Shakespeare, reportedly 'encountered a barrage of opposition to *The Songlines*, especially from academics and activists' (Thubron 1999), particularly on the basis that Chatwin had misrepresented crucial aspects of Aboriginal belief, and that he had violated the trust of those who had shared with him 'sacred knowledge'.
16. A detailed consideration of various pages in Chatwin suggests the nature of this slippage between the terms 'nomad', 'pastoralist' and 'hunter-gatherer' (see Chatwin 1988: 21, 50, 56, 129, 131, 184, 191, 192–93, 201, 202, 271).
17. It has been suggested that the figure of Arkady was modelled at least in part on Salman Rushdie who accompanied Chatwin on some of his Australian travels. However, Rushdie denies this, claiming that there was a more obvious model in Alice Springs (Murray 1993: 89).

Chapter 2: My Pen is the Tongue of a Skilful Poet

1. Anderson, too, notes that national anthems or songs may be powerful '[n]o matter how banal the words and mediocre the tunes' (1991: 145).
2. Nontsizi Mgqwetho's work was discovered in its archival locations by Jeff Opland. With the assistance of Phyllis Ntantala and Abner Nyamende he has collated and translated the poems and prose pieces; the collection of Mgqwetho's writing is lodged in the Opland Collection of Xhosa Literature.

3. See, for example, Thabo Mbeki's plea to priests 'to pray for God to enter our hearts and minds so that there is peace' prior to the 14 April 2004 elections (Lombard et al. 2004), or the South African Football Association president, Molefi Oliphant, saying before the announcement of the host country for the 2010 soccer World Cup, 'We are now leaving everything in the hands of God' ('Manuel Set to Toot his Horn the Loudest' 2004).
4. The 2001 census figures for religious affiliation are as follows: Christianity 79.6%, 15.1% no religion, 1.5% Islam, 1.2% Hinduism, 0.2% Judaism, 0.3% African traditional, 1.4% undetermined, and 0.6% other faiths (Kane-Berman et al. 2004: 28). The biggest increase in the period 1980–2001 has been in the Zion Christian Churches, with membership up by 546.8% (Kane-Berman et al. 2004: 29). The percentage of people by race group identifying themselves as Christians in 1990 was as follows: 92.1% of whites, 86% of Coloureds, 76% of Africans, and 13% of Indians (Elphick 1997b: 1).
5. 'A colonisation of consciousness' is the term used by the Comaroffs in their influential study (1991: 250).
6. Bosch points to the importance of such church communities for Christianity worldwide: 'These churches, together with similar Christian movements among other . . . societies . . . may indeed be seen as the fifth major Christian church type, after the eastern Orthodox churches, the Roman Catholic Church, the Protestant Reformation, and the Pentecostal churches' (quoted in Pretorius and Jafta 1997: 211). Pretorius and Jafta suggest that: 'How the mainline churches respond to the [African Initiated Churches] may be one of the most significant ecclesiastical issues for the next century' (1997: 226).
7. Certain of Mgqwetho's poems appear in Opland and Mtuze's *Izwi labantu* (1994), Chapman's *New Century of South African Poetry* (2002), and in the anthology *Women Writing Africa* (Daymond et al. 2003).
8. The poem appeared in *Umteteli wa Bantu* on 12 January 1924.
9. It has a similar endnote to the 1998 translation describing Mgqwetho's verbal abilities.
10. From this point onwards, Mgqwetho's poems and articles from *Umteteli wa Bantu* will be referenced by the date of publication only.
11. The biographical information that follows has been gleaned from Opland's biographical summary (2005), as well as from my own close readings of the poems and articles.
12. As her first publication in *Umteteli wa Bantu* was on 23 October 1920 there is a clear suggestion that she had been either performing or publishing prior to appearing in Maxeke's newspaper.

13. See Opland (2005).
14. See Attwell (2005) for a discussion of the debate between Dhlomo and Vilakazi on this subject.
15. S.E.K. Mqhayi also published poems marking Christmas and New Year in newspapers.
16. See Mweli Skota (1931: 441).
17. See Mweli Skota (1931); Mills (1997: 346); Elphick (1997a: 357); and Pretorius and Jafta (1997: 215).
18. De Kock is, of course, discussing missionisation in the late nineteenth century, when the social space for African-Christian agency was more circumscribed. The movement beyond 'agonism' or 'permanent provocation' may reflect the changed historical circumstances of people such as Mgqwetho in the 1920s, in particular their greater independence from mission influence.
19. Moravian missions emphasised especially self-control and the gospel of work. For example, the Regulations of the Congregation at Genadendal (drawn up and agreed to by all the inhabitants in 1816) included the following: 'The object of the Brethren's living together in separate settlements is, that they may as much as possible be out of the way of temptations, and that by the preaching of the word of God connected with a wholesome Church discipline a living knowledge of Jesus Christ, and a godly way of life may be promoted among the inhabitants' (Hofmeyr et al. 1994: 76); 'We consider drunkenness as a great sin, which is frequently the occasion of exciting the worst passion . . .'; and 'No one is permitted to bring spiritous liquors from other places to Genadendal, and all plays of a mischievous and immoral tendency are prohibited' (Hofmeyr et al. 1994: 77).
20. Hofmeyr's fascinating study, *The Portable Bunyan: A Transnational History of* The Pilgrim's Progress, has a brief discussion of the influence of Bunyan in this poem (2004: 132–34).

Chapter 3: 'Structures of Feeling' and Constructions of History

1. See Hamilton (1998) and Wylie (1999, 2006) for detailed analysis of some of the conflicting images of Shaka.
2. Kunene claims the veracity of his representation over that of Thomas Mofolo ('My *Shaka* is more historical. Mofolo's is just myth' [Wilkinson 1992: 140]) and others ('So my *Shaka* is more authentic, definitely' [Wilkinson 1992: 141]).

3. From this point onwards, references to *Emperor Shaka the Great* will be made by page numbers only.
4. A photocopy of the original Zulu manuscript is lodged in the Harry Ransom Center at the University of Texas in Austin. I located an incomplete version of the Zulu manuscript (comprising about two-thirds of the epic) in a storeroom in the Campbell Collections at the University of KwaZulu-Natal in Durban. A detailed comparative analysis of these manuscripts with Kunene's English translation is beyond my abilities as critic, though a superficial comparison suggests that the Zulu and English texts are indeed rather different. Ernest Mathabela's Ph.D. thesis provides a detailed engagement with the Ransom Center manuscript.
5. This strategy does not always seem to me to be successful. Kunene's use of terms such as 'foreign potentate' (65) or 'gangster kings' (103) sometimes risks historical incongruity or anachronism.
6. Personal communication with the author.
7. Kunene says about the literary education he received from his parents: 'So there was a kind of very deep critique of how you put things in a language. Literature was very important: it was not just literature for its own sake, it was history, politics, the philosophy of society and everything. So through history and through literature they were training their own children about various aspects of life including ethics' (Wilkinson 1992: 138).
8. See Brown (1998: 104–06) for a discussion of these developments in the form of *izibongo*.
9. See Opland (1984) for a discussion of these debates.
10. Some examples of these formulae include: 'The dawn was the brilliant eye of morning' (20); 'Dawn speared eternally from the horizon' (34); 'The delicate scent of meat rose in waves to the heavens' (80); and 'the morning came, with her children, from the mountains' (221).
11. It is unclear to what extent the echoes of *Macbeth* are a result of Kunene's familiarity with the Zulu stage production of *Macbeth*, *Umabatha* (first performed in 1970).
12. Ari Sitas makes an analogous point: 'The result is a poetry dislocated from the immediate structures of feeling and the rhythms of resistance of a modern day industrial proletariat . . .' (1994: 146).
13. Wylie (1999, 2006), however, argues that accounts of Shaka's innovative methods of warfare, particularly the introduction of the stabbing spear, have little evidentiary basis.
14. Kunene claims that 'Palm Race' is a mythological appellation for the Zulu nation, signifying – through the image of a single tree with many

trunks – multiplicity within a broader unity (personal communication with the author).

15. Notwithstanding the poem's reliance in its sources on women's oral testimony, within Kunene's patriarchal social conception the narrator is clearly male.
16. See Liz Gunner (1984) and Jeff Guy (1994).

Chapter 4: Environment and Identity

1. See Chapman (1981, 1984).
2. A recent MA thesis has explored these issues further (Stevens 2004).
3. Klopper says about 'The Lost Mine', for example: 'The bats that sew up the seam of conflict, and hence resolve it on a symbolic level, actively repress history' (1990: 288).
4. 'If you care to describe its legs, I will try to tell you about my relationship with it', he once responded memorably to a question about his relationship with 'the literary establishment' (Brown and Van Dyk 1991: 40).
5. From this point onwards, references to *A Littoral Zone* will be by page numbers only.
6. Personal communication with the author.
7. Livingstone has constantly rejected the idea that animals have no emotional/spiritual sense, while refusing the temptation of anthropomorphism. See, for example, his critique of Ted Hughes (Chapman 1985: 98).
8. Personal communication with the author.
9. This point is well illustrated by Appiah: '[T]he chances of two people who are both "Caucasoid" differing in genetic constitution at one site on a given chromosome are about 14.3 percent, while, for any two people taken at random from the human population, they are about 14.8 percent' (1992: 36).
10. In 'The Explainer', Livingstone says:

        Forgiveness I ask

    for not shutting up after
    knowledge, for not confining
    myself to chimneys or to the

    Cyclon B. Incapable of
    a talented silence: doing
    my thing on birds and beasts of this earth

is to watch myself in case
I wake behind barbed wire, holstered
with authority, jackboots on. (1981: 38)

Chapter 5: Narrative, Memory and Mapping

1. From this point onwards, references to the short stories in *'At the Edge' and Other Cato Manor Stories* will be made by page numbers only.
2. I think the reference to 'the sixties' is inaccurate, as none of the stories seems to move beyond the late 1950s in its narrative period.
3. Rushdie, for example, stresses the value of leaving home and crossing frontiers (linguistic, intellectual, imaginative, racial and geographic), of learning that 'once we have left our childhood places and started to make up our own lives, armed only with what we have and are, we understand . . . that there is no longer any such place as home; except, of course, for the home we make' (Lee 2003).
4. Robert Young (2001) makes this point, as does Michael Chapman (2003).
5. My initial interest in the correlation of the form of the stories with the map was sparked by a colleague Michael Green, who explored some of these ideas in relation to the story 'The Incomplete Human Being' in a first-year module entitled 'Language, Text and Context'. We developed the module with several other colleagues from the Faculty of Human Sciences at what was then the University of Natal, and taught it for the first time in 1998.
6. See Brown (1998: 167–68).
7. Govender's comments raise the vexed question of an appropriate orthography for dialect/patois. The common term for smoking a marijuana cigarette, the Afrikaans-derived 'skyfing', becomes in Govender's stories 'skafing' (131) (*A Dictionary of South African English* opts for 'skyf' or the variant 'skuif', though Mesthrie's *A Lexicon of South African Indian English* offers 'skafe'); 'waai' (the Afrikaans slang for 'go') becomes 'vie' (*A Dictionary of South African English* suggests also the 'Englished forms vy, vye'); Govender's 'pozzie' is 'pozi' in Mesthrie; and the patois/dialect rendering of 'fellows' is not 'fellahs' but, curiously, 'fullahs' (in *The Lahnee's Pleasure*, the only one of Govender's plays to have been published, the script uses the even stranger 'fullers'). It remains uncertain whether Govender's orthography reflects an attempt at more accurate phonetic spellings, or a tactic to downplay English/Afrikaans cross-cultural influences in South African Indian speech patterns (the

motive for the latter, if this is indeed the case, might be 'black' solidarity in the anti-apartheid struggle).

8. We could compare the response of the *Drum* writers of the 1950s to the destruction of Sophiatown.
9. Isabel Hofmeyr suggested this idea to me.

Chapter 6: 'Who's that Black Boys Making that Black Noise . . .'

1. An example of academic discourse that seems to me far too stolid for its subject-matter is the following section, from an article on hip-hop spray-can art, in which Klopper quotes Erasmus and Pieterse:

   > 'It is important to conceptualise coloured identities as relational identities shaped by complex networks of concrete social relations rather than seeing "coloured" as a particular category of individuals and/or simply an imposed name from a racist past.' The value of this approach, they argue, 'is its challenge to any notions of colouredness as homogenous and/or an essentialist ethnic identity with fixed cultural boundaries as well as its acknowledgement of the particularity of identities.' (2000: 193)

2. The album sleeve of *Ghetto Code* (1997) includes pictures of band members with, amongst others, James Brown, Quincy Jones and Ice Cube.
3. Both Haupt and Watkins also draw on Rose's approach.
4. One of the strongly anti-valorising statements quoted by Watkins is the following from Emile:

   > Sometimes we perform at shows and I wonder what the fuck am I doing here, like the show for the Olympics. I didn't support the bid but we were performing there and I was so relieved when we didn't get it. We appear in the show because they pay us and we didn't care a fuck . . . it is just our money anyway that they blew like that . . . life would have been unbearable in this place. (Watkins 2000: 100)

5. According to Lance Stehr fifteen tracks from the album were banned for lyrical content, as was the video for 'Understand Where I'm Coming From', probably because it contained unrest footage (personal communication).
6. The English translation provided here and in Notes 7, 9, 11, 12 and 13

is literal and does not attempt to capture the play of rhythm and rhyme in the originals:

My face is as black as the night
And you stand and laugh
With your power you have raped our people
You have forgotten about the day of the covenant
My weapon is my mouth
And it will explode like a bomb.

7. Unity is strength, I want to laugh
because a whole race, regardless of gender
is waiting for freedom.

8. Watkins talks of moving beyond Rose's model 'by suggesting that hip-hop style is, more definitively, about the blending and juxtaposition of differences', what he calls 'texture' (2000: 130–31). While I agree that 'texture' is indeed an important aspect of hip-hop, it seems to me that 'texture' often constitutes simply a subtle, or stark, form of Rose's layering, and rupture.

9. My little brother was shot right through his head
Because there was a gang fight on our block
The fight started because of an argument about a drink and a pipe
Suddenly someone grabbed a stick
A bottle was broken, a young guy was stabbed
Before he knew it another one was shot . . . .

10. A more thoroughgoing analysis of Cape hip-hop and Islam would nevertheless be enlightening.

11. 'I'm talking about a maid' (see Note 12).

12. The English translation of 'meit' is 'maid'. Both 'maid' and 'meit' were terms used in apartheid society by white employers to refer, in a patronising, derogatory or dismissive way, to black, female domestic workers.

13. Or are you looking for a father for your kid
You're acting hoity-toity
But that's not alright
What I mean to say
You were willing to sleep with me
But now you want to give me a scare
'Cause the baby is there
I may be a dad, a father
But Ramone was there too
Don't complain, I'm not a fool
Nine months ago I wasn't even in the Cape

It's tough, you haven't got a case
Shut your mouth, don't even talk
Because you can't do anything
Enough of that
I'm talking about a maid
. . .
You're stuck up, you're fucked up and what
What, do you think you're white with your black twat . . .

Select Bibliography

Abrams, M.H. 1981. *A Glossary of Literary Terms*. New York: Holt, Rinehart and Winston.

Adams, Catherine. 1998. 'Cannibal Chutney a Matter of Taste.' *Mail and Guardian* 27 November–3 December.

Anderson, Benedict. 1991 [1983]. *Imagined Communities: Reflections on the Origin and Spread of Nationalism*. London: Verso.

Appiah, Kwame Anthony. 1992. *In My Father's House: Africa in the Philosophy of Culture*. New York: Oxford University Press.

Attwell, David. 2005. *Rewriting Modernity: Studies in Black South African Literary History*. Pietermaritzburg: University of KwaZulu-Natal Press.

Barnett, Antony. 2002. 'Fat Windfall for the San.' *Mail and Guardian* 5–11 April.

Barnett, Ursula A. 1983. *A Vision of Order: A Study of Black South African Literature in English (1914–1980)*. London: Sinclair Browne; Amherst: University of Massachusetts Press; and Cape Town: Maskew Miller Longman.

Beadle, Jeremy J. 1993. *Will Pop Eat Itself? Pop Music in the Soundbite Era*. London: Faber.

Beckett, Denis. 1996. *Trekking: In Search of the Real South Africa*. Johannesburg: Penguin.

Bhabha, Homi K. 1990. 'DissemiNation: Time, Narrative, and the Margins of the Modern Nation'. In *Nation and Narration*, ed. Homi K. Bhabha, 291–322. London and New York: Routledge.

Bleek, W.H.I. and L.C. Lloyd. 1911. *Specimens of Bushman Folklore*. London: George Allen and Co.

Borger, Julian. 1999. 'Inuits Get their Promised Land.' *Mail and Guardian* 26 March–1 April.

Brown, Duncan. 1992. 'Interview with Mongane Wally Serote.' *Theoria* 80 (October): 143–49.

———. 1998. *Voicing the Text: South African Oral Poetry and Performance*. Cape Town: Oxford University Press.

Brown, Duncan and Bruno van Dyk (eds.). 1991. *Exchanges: South African Writing in Transition*. Pietermaritzburg: University of Natal Press.

Césaire, Aimé. 1969. *Return to my Native Land.* Translated by John Berger and Anna Bostock. Introduction by Mazisi Kunene. Harmondsworth: Penguin.

Chakrabarty, Dipesh. 2000. *Provincialising Europe: Postcolonial Thought and Historical Difference*. Princeton and Oxford: Princeton University Press.

Chamberlin, J. Edward. 1998. 'Doing Things with Words: Putting Performance on the Page.' *Voices* 1: 5–27.

———. 1999. 'Hunting, Tracking and Reading.' Seminar paper delivered at the University of Natal, Durban.

———. 2002. 'Hunting, Tracking and Reading.' In *Literacy, Narrative and Culture*, ed. Jens Brockmeier, David R. Olson and Min Wang, 67–85. London: Curzon Press.

———. 2003. *If this is Your Land, Where are Your Stories? Finding Common Ground.* Toronto: Knopf Canada.

Chapman, Michael. 1981. *Douglas Livingstone: A Critical Study of his Poetry*. Johannesburg: Ad. Donker.

———. 1984. *South African English Poetry: A Modern Perspective*. Johannesburg: Ad. Donker.

———. 1985. 'The Science of Poetry and the Poetry of Science.' *English Academy Review* 3: 89–101.

———. 2003 [1996] *Southern African Literatures*. Pietermaritzburg: University of KwaZulu-Natal Press.

Chapman, Michael (ed.). 1990. *The Drum Decade*. Pietermaritzburg: University of Natal Press.

———. 2002. *The New Century of South African Poetry*. Johannesburg: Ad. Donker.

Chatwin, Bruce. 1988 [1987]. *The Songlines*. London: Jonathan Cape.

Chetty, Rajendra. 2002. 'Interview with Ronnie Govender.' In *South African Indian Writings in English*, ed. Rajendra Chetty, 337–46. Durban: Institute for Black Research/Madiba Publishers.

Clingman, Stephen. 2004. 'Bram Fischer and the Question of Identity.' *Current Writing* 16(1): 61–79.

Comaroff, Jean and John Comaroff. 1991. *Of Revelation and Revolution: Christianity, Colonialism and Consciousness in South Africa*. Vol.1. Chicago: University of Chicago Press.

Darian-Smith, Kate, Liz Gunner and Sarah Nuttall (eds.). 1996. *Text, Theory and Space: Land, Literature and History in South African and Australia*. London and New York: Routledge.

Daymond, Margaret, Dorothy Driver, Sheila Meintjies, Leloba Molema, Chiedza Musengezi, Margie Orford and Nobantu Rasebotsa (eds.). 2003. *Women Writing Africa: The Southern Region*. Johannesburg: Witwatersrand University Press.

De Certeau, Michel. 1988 [1984]. *The Practice of Everyday Life*. Translated by Steven Randall. Los Angeles: University of California Press.

De Certeau, Michel and Luce Giard. 1998. 'The Practical Science of the Singular: Orality, Operativity and the Ordinary.' In *The Practice of Everyday Life. Vol. 2: Living and Cooking*, eds. Michael de Certeau, Luce Giard and Pierre Mayol, 251–56. Minneapolis: University of Minnesota Press.

Decker, Jeffrey Louis. 1993. 'The State of Rap: Time and Place in Hip-Hop Nationalism.' *Social Text* 34 (Spring): 53–84.

De Kock, Leon. 1996. *Civilising Barbarians: Missionary Narrative and African Textual Response in Nineteenth-Century South Africa*. Johannesburg: Witwatersrand University Press.

De Villiers, Bertus (ed.). 1997. *The Rights of Indigenous People: A Quest for Coexistence*. Pretoria: Human Sciences Research Council.

De Vries, Fred. 1993. 'Confrontation in the *Age of Truth*.' *Mail and Guardian* 19–26 November.

Dorsey, David. 1988. 'Critical Perceptions of African Poetry.' *African Literature Today* 16: 26–38.

Duerden, Denis and Cosmo Pieterse (eds.). 1982. *African Writers Talking*. London: Heinemann.

Eco, Umberto. 1984 [1983]. *The Name of the Rose*. London: Picador.

Elphick, Richard. 1997a. 'The Benevolent Empire and the Social Gospel: Missionaries and South African Christians in the Age of Segregation.' In *Christianity in South Africa: A Political, Social and Cultural History*, ed. Richard Elphick and Rodney Davenport, 347–69. Oxford: James Currey and Cape Town: David Philip.

———. 1997b. 'Introduction: Christianity in South African History.' In *Christianity in South Africa: A Political, Social and Cultural History*, ed. Richard Elphick and Rodney Davenport, 1–15. Oxford: James Currey and Cape Town: David Philip.

Erlmann, Veit. 1996. *Nightsong: Performance, Power and Practice in South Africa*. Chicago: University of Chicago Press.

Eyal, Dror. 2000. 'Cape Town's Hip-Hop Scene.' http://www.rage.co.za. Accessed on 20/7/2000.

Fazzini, Marco. 1991. 'Interviewing Douglas Livingstone.' *New Contrast*, 74 & 75/19(2 & 3): 135–45.

Feldman, Peter. 1997. 'South Africa's Most Talented Seers.' *The Star* 22 May.

Forgey, Herma, Tamara Dimant, Terence Corrigan, Thabo Mophuthing, Jessica Spratt, Daniel Pienaar, Nyanisile Peter and Ellen Potter. 2001. *South Africa Survey 2000/2001*. Johannesburg: South African Institute of Race Relations.

Foster, Craig and Damon Foster. 2000. *The Great Dance*. Aaardvark, Earthrise, Liquid Pictures and Off the Fence.

Friedman, Hazel. 1998. 'How Gangs Tore out a Community's Heart.' *Sunday Independent* 22 February.

Gabriëlse, Ramses. 2002. 'There is no Freedom in this Country.' *Mail and Guardian* 11–17 October.

Gaitskell, Deborah. 1997. 'Power in Prayer and Service: Women's Christian Organisations.' In *Christianity in South Africa: A Political, Social and Cultural History*, ed. Richard Elphick and Rodney Davenport, 253–67. Oxford: James Currey and Cape Town: David Philip.

Gates, Henry Louis. 1987. *Figures in Black: Words, Signs and the 'Racial' Self.* New York and Oxford: Oxford University Press.

———. 1988. *The Signifying Monkey: A Theory of African-American Literary Criticism*. New York and London: Oxford University Press.

George, Nelson. 1998. *Hip Hop America*. New York: Viking Penguin.

Gérard, Albert S. 1981. *African Language Literatures*. Harlow: Longman.

Gierach, John. 2002 [1988]. *Death, Taxes and Leaky Waders*. London: Robinson.

Goodwin, Ken. 1982. *Understanding African Poetry*. London: Heinemann.

Gordon, Robert. 1992. *The Bushman Myth: The Making of a Namibian Underclass*. Boulder and Oxford: Westview Press.

Govender, Ronnie. 1996. *'At the Edge' and Other Cato Manor Stories*. Pretoria: Manx.

———. 2001. *The Lahnee's Pleasure*. Johannesburg: Ravan Press.

Gowans, Jill. 2002a. 'The Art of Survival through the Ages.' *Sunday Tribune (Perspectives)* 20 January.

———. 2002b. 'Respect will Save Rock Art Heritage.' *Sunday Tribune (Perspectives)* 20 January.

Gray, Derek. 1996. 'Death of Poet is Great Loss to City.' *Daily News* 29 February.

Guenther, Mathias G. 1989. *Bushman Folktales: Oral Traditions of the Nharo of Botswana and the /Xam of the Cape*. Stuttgart: Franz Steiner Verlag Wiesbaden GMBH.

Gunner, Liz. 1984. '*Ukubonga Nezibongo:* Zulu Praising and Praises.' Ph.D. dissertation, School of Oriental and African Studies, University of London.

———. 1996. 'Names and the Land: Poetry of Belonging and Unbelonging, a Comparative Approach.' In *Text, Theory and Space: Land, Literature and*

History in South Africa and Australia, eds. Kate Darian-Smith, Liz Gunner and Sarah Nuttall, 115–30. London and New York: Routledge.

Guy, Jeff. 1994 [1979]. *The Destruction of the Zulu Kingdom*. Pietermaritzburg: University of Natal Press.

Habermas, Jurgen. 1989 [1962]. *The Structural Transformation of the Public Sphere: An Inquiry into a Category of Bourgeois Society*. Translated by Thomas Burger. Cambridge, Massachusetts: MIT Press.

Hamilton, Carolyn. 1998. *Terrific Majesty: The Powers of Shaka Zulu and the Limits of the Historical Imagination*. Cape Town: David Philip.

Haupt, Adam. 1995. 'Rap and the Articulation of Resistance: An Exploration of Subversive Cultural Production during the Early Nineties, with Particular Reference to Prophets of da City.' Masters thesis, University of the Western Cape, Cape Town.

———. 1996. 'Stifled Noise in the South African Music Box: Prophets of da City and the Struggle for Public Space.' *South African Theatre Journal* 10(2) (September): 51–61.

———. 2001. 'Black Thing: Hip-Hop Nationalism, "Race" and Gender in Prophets of da City and Brasse vannie Kaap.' In *Coloured by History, Shaped by Place: New Perspectives on Coloured Identities in Cape Town*, ed. Zimitri Erasmus, 173–91. Cape Town: Kwela.

Haynes, John. 1987. *African Poetry and the English Language*. London: Macmillan.

Heaney, Seamus. 1972. *Wintering Out*. London: Faber.

Herbert, Ross. 1998. 'Dumped in a Bleak New Home, the San Try to Cling to their Culture.' *Sunday Independent* 29 March.

Hewitt, Roger. 1986. *Structure, Meaning and Ritual in the Narratives of the Southern San*. Hamburg: Helmut Buske Verlag.

'Hip Hop and Rap Blamed.' 2000. *Sunday Tribune* 23 July.

Hodgson, Janet. 1997. 'A Battle for Sacred Power: Christian Beginnings among the Xhosa.' In *Christianity in South Africa: A Political, Social and Cultural History*, ed. Richard Elphick and Rodney Davenport, 68–88. Oxford: James Currey and Cape Town: David Philip.

Hofmeyr, Isabel. 1993. *'We Spend our Years as a Tale that is Told': Oral Historical Narrative in a South African Chiefdom*. Johannesburg: Witwatersrand University Press.

———. 1995. '"Wailing for Purity": Oral Studies in Southern African Studies.' *African Studies* 54 (2): 16–31.

———. 2004. *The Portable Bunyan: A Transnational History of* The Pilgrim's Progress. Princeton and Oxford: Princeton University Press.

Hofmeyr, J.W., J.A. Millard and C.J.J. Froneman (eds.). 1994 [1991]. *History of the Church in South Africa: A Document and Source Book*. Pretoria: UNISA.

http://www.rucus.ac.za/-eitan/poc (accessed on 18 April 2000).

Jameson, Fredric. 1988. 'Marxism and Historicism.' In *The Ideologies of Theory: Essays 1971–1986: Volume 2: The Syntax of History*, 149–77. London: Routledge.

Jordan, Bobby. 1998. 'Bushmen on the Spoor to Nowhere.' *Sunday Times* 31 May.

Juluka. 1981. *African Litany*. Music Incorporated (Minc records).

Kane-Berman, John, Jane Tempest, Frans Cronjé, Tamara Dimant, Kerwin Lebone, Marco MacFarlane, Michael Cardo and Nick Ericsson. 2004. *South Africa Survey 2003/2004*. Johannesburg: South African Institute of Race Relations.

Klopper, Dirk. 1990. 'Ideology and the Study of White South African English Poetry.' In *Rendering Things Visible: Essays on South African Literary Culture of the 1970s and 1980s*, ed. Martin Trump, 256–94. Johannesburg: Ravan Press.

Klopper, Sandra. 2000. 'Hip-Hop Graffiti Art'. In *Senses of Culture: South African Cultural Studies*, eds. Sarah Nuttall and Cheryl-Ann Michael, 178–96. Cape Town: Oxford University Press.

Krog, Antjie. 2003. *A Change of Tongue*. Johannesburg: Random House.

Kunene, Mazisi. 1970. *Zulu Poems*. London: Deutsch.

———. 1979. *Emperor Shaka the Great: A Zulu Epic*. London: Heinemann.

———. 1981. *Anthem of the Decades*. London: Heinemann.

———. 1982. *The Ancestors and the Sacred Mountain*. London: Heinemann.

Lee, Hermione. 2003. 'Border Wars' (Review of Salman Rushdie's *Step Across this Line: Collected Non-Fiction 1992–2002*). *Mail and Guardian* 31 January–6 February.

Liebenberg, Louis. 1990. *The Art of Tracking: The Origin of Science*. Cape Town: David Philip.

Livingstone, D.J. 1986. 'Science and Truth.' *Transactions of the Royal Society of South Africa* 46(2) (December): 99–107.

———. 1989. 'A Microbial Study of Water Quality in the Marine Environment off Durban: 1964–1988.' Ph.D. dissertation, Department of Biology, University of Natal, Durban.

Livingstone, Douglas. 1960. *The Skull in the Mud*. Dulwich: Outposts Publications.

———. 1976. '"Africa within us". . . .' In *Poetry South Africa: Selected Papers from Poetry '74*, eds. Peter Wilhelm and James A. Polley, 142–44. Johannesburg: Ad. Donker.

———. 1977. 'A Rhino for the Boardroom.' In *Contemporary South African Plays*, ed. Ernest Pereira, 20–58. Johannesburg: Ravan Press.

———. 1978. *The Anvil's Undertone*. Johannesburg: Ad. Donker.

———. 1981 [1970]. *Eyes Closed against the Sun*. Cape Town: Oxford University Press.

———. 1982. 'The Poetry of Mtshali, Serote, Sepamla and Others in English: Notes towards a Critical Evaluation.' In *Soweto Poetry*, ed. Michael Chapman, 157–61. Johannesburg: McGraw-Hill.

———. 1983 [1975]. *A Rosary of Bone*. Cape Town: David Philip.

———. 1988 [1964]. *Sjambok and other Poems from Africa*. Johannesburg: Ad. Donker.

———. 1991. *A Littoral Zone*. Cape Town: Carrefour Press.

Lombard, Edwin, Xolisa Vapi and Bongani Mthethwa. 2004. 'Mbeki Appeals to Voters and God.' *Sunday Times* 11 April.

Machen, Peter. 2000. 'Music was the Loser at Splashy Fen.' *Sunday Tribune Magazine* 7 May.

Madingoane, Ingoapele. 1979. *africa my beginning*. Johannesburg: Ravan Press.

Magnette. 1997. 'Knowing your Roots.' *Epic*. Photocopy courtesy of Ghetto Ruff Records.

Malaba, Mbongeni Z. 1988. 'Super-Shaka: Mazisi Kunene's *Emperor Shaka the Great*.' *Research in African Literatures* 19(4) (Winter): 477–88.

Mandela, Nelson. 1995 [1994]. *Long Walk to Freedom*. London: Abacus.

'Manuel Set to Toot his Horn the Loudest.' *The Witness* 13 May 2004.

Mathabela, Earnest. 1991. 'Myth, History, and Politics in Mazisi Kunene's Epic Poetry.' Ph.D. thesis, University of Texas, Austin.

Mesthrie, Rajend. 1992a. *English Language in Shift: The History, Structure and Sociolinguistics of South African Indian English*. Cambridge: Cambridge University Press.

———. 1992b. *A Lexicon of South African Indian English*. Leeds: Papal Tree.

Miller, Christopher. 1990. *Theories of Africans: Francophone Literature and Anthropology in Africa*. Chicago and London: University of Chicago Press.

Mills, Wallace G. 1997. 'Millennial Christianity, British Imperialism and the Social Gospel.' In *Christianity in South Africa: A Political, Social and Cultural History*, ed. Richard Elphick and Rodney Davenport, 337–46. Oxford: James Currey and Cape Town: David Philip.

Mitchell, Grant. 1999. 'A Lesson in Sharing from America's First Nations.' *Sunday Independent* 10 January.

Mkondo, Rich. 1998. 'The Trail of Tears in the United States.' *Daily News* 12 May.

Mphahlele, Es'kia. 1987. 'The Tyranny of Place and Aesthetics: The South African Case.' In *Race and Literature*, ed. Charles Malan, 48–59. Pinetown: Owen Burgess.

Murray, Nicholas. 1993. *Bruce Chatwin*. Bridgend: Seren Books.

Mutloatse, Mothobi (ed.). 1980. *Forced Landing*. Johannesburg: Ravan Press.

Mweli Skota, T.D. 1931. *The African Yearly Register: Being an Illustrated National Biographical Dictionary (Who's Who) of Black Folks in Africa*. Johannesburg: R.L. Esson and Co.

Narismulu, Priya. 1986. 'Douglas Livingstone's Poems: Expressions of an Understanding of One's Reality.' *AUETSA Papers* Vol. 2: 296–316.

Negus, Keith. 1998. 'Cultural Production and the Corporation: Musical Genres and the Strategic Management of Creativity in the US Recording Industry.' *Media, Culture and Society* 20: 359–79.

Ong, Walter J. 1982. *Orality and Literacy: The Technologizing of the Word*. London and New York: Methuen.

Opland, Jeff. 1983. *Xhosa Oral Poetry: Aspects of a Black South African Tradition*. Johannesburg: Ravan Press.

———. 1984. 'The Transition from Oral to Written Literature: Areas of Research into South African Bantu Languages.' In *SA Literature Research*, ed. Charles Malan, 109–20. Pretoria: Human Sciences Research Council.

———. 1997. 'The Drumbeat of the Cross: Christianity and Literature.' In *Christianity in South Africa: A Political, Social and Cultural History*, ed. Richard Elphick and Rodney Davenport, 297–318. Oxford: James Currey and Cape Town: David Philip.

———. 1998. *Xhosa Poets and Poetry*. Cape Town: David Philip.

———. 1999. 'The Image of the Book in Xhosa Oral Poetry.' In *Oral Literature and Performance in Southern Africa*, ed. Duncan Brown, 90–110. Oxford: James Currey; Cape Town: David Philip; and Athens: Ohio University Press.

Opland, Jeff and Peter Tshobisa Mtuze (eds.). 1994. *Izwi labantu*. Cape Town: Oxford University Press.

Opland, Jeff, with Peter Mtuze and Phyllis Ntantala (trans. and eds.). 2005. *Ah, the Grief that Seizes your Country, Nontsizi! The Xhosa Poetry of Nontsizi Mgqwetho*. Surrey: Unpublished Manuscript.

Pretorius, Hennie and Lizo Jafta. 1997. '"A Branch Springs Out": African Initiated Churches.' In *Christianity in South Africa: A Political, Social and Cultural History*, ed. Richard Elphick and Rodney Davenport, 211–26. Oxford: James Currey and Cape Town: David Philip.

Prophets of da City. 1990. *Our World*. Ghetto Ruff/Teal Trutone.

———. 1992. *Boomstyle*. Ghetto Ruff/Teal Trutone.

———. 1993. *Age of Truth*. Ghetto Ruff/Tusk Records.

———. 1994. *Phunk Phlow*. Ghetto Ruff/Teal Trutone.

———. 1995. *Universal Souljaz*. Beggars Banquet, UK.

———. 1997. *Ghetto Code*. Ghetto Ruff/Polygram Records.

Public Enemy. 1988. *It Takes a Nation of Millions to Hold us Back*. Simply Vinyl.

———. 1990. *Fear of a Black Planet*. Def Jam.

Quayson, Ato. 1995. 'Orality – (Theory) – Textuality: Tutuola, Okri and the Relationship of Literary Practice to Oral Traditions.' In *The Pressures of the Text: Orality, Texts and the Telling of Tales*, ed. Stewart Brown, 96–117. Birmingham: Centre of West African Studies, Birmingham University.

Reed, Christopher. 1998. 'Conservation Group Clashes with Indian Tribe over Whales.' *Mail and Guardian* 9–15 October.

Rose, Tricia. 1994. *Black Noise: Rap Music and Black Culture in Contemporary America*. Hanover and London: Wesleyan University Press.

Rouse, Rose. 1995. 'Proud and Positive.' Source unknown. Photocopy courtesy of Ghetto Ruff Records.

Ryan, Simon. 1994. 'Inscribing the Emptiness: Cartography, Exploration and the Construction of Australia.' In *De-scribing Empire: Postcolonialism and Textuality*, ed. Chris Tiffin and Alan Lawson, 115–30. London: Routledge.

Schumacher, Thomas G. 1995. '"This is a Sampling Sport": Digital Sampling, Rap Music and the Law in Cultural Production.' *Media, Culture and Society* 17: 253–73.

Segal, Lynne. 1998. 'Battle to Find a Common Language to Give Vanishing Cultures a Voice'. *Sunday Independent* 10 May.

Serote, Mongane Wally. 1972. *Yakhal'inkomo*. Johannesburg: Renoster.

Sesay, Kodiatu. 1988. 'Hopes of a Harvest Festival.' *African Literature Today* 16: 61–76.

Silva, Penny, Wendy Dore, Dorothea Mantzel, Colin Muller and Madeleine Wright (eds.). 1996. *Dictionary of South African English on Historical Principles*. Oxford: Oxford University Press.

Sitas, Ari. 1994. 'Traditions of Poetry in Natal.' In *Politics and Performance: Theatre, Poetry and Song in Southern Africa*, ed. Liz Gunner, 139–61. Johannesburg: Witwatersrand University Press.

Stapleton, Katrina R. 1998. 'From the Margins to Mainstream: The Political Power of Hip-Hop.' *Media, Culture and Society* 20: 219–34.

Stevens, Mariss Patricia. 2004. '"Symbiosis or Death": An Ecocritical Examination of Douglas Livingstone's Poetry.' Masters thesis, Rhodes University, Grahamstown.

The Holy Bible: New International Version. 1994 [1973]. Cape Town: Bible Society of South Africa.

Thompson, Elizabeth. 1986. 'An Interview with Douglas Livingstone.' *Crux* (October): 3–12.

Thubron, Colin. 1999. 'Sobering but Empathetic Account of a Restless Spirit Prowling the Perimeter.' *Sunday Independent* 16 May.

Toop, David. 1984. *The Rap Attack: African Jive to New York Hip Hop*. London: Pluto.

Walshe, Peter. 1997. 'Christianity and the Anti-Apartheid Struggle: The Prophetic Voice within Divided Churches.' In *Christianity in South Africa: A Political, Social and Cultural History*, ed. Richard Elphick and Rodney Davenport, 383–99. Oxford: James Currey and Cape Town: David Philip.

Watkins, Lee William. 2000. 'Tracking the Narrative: The Poetics of Identity in Rap Music and Hip-Hop Culture in Cape Town.' Masters thesis, University of Natal, Durban.

Weaver, Tony. 2002. 'De Beers Warning on San Action.' *Daily News* 20 November.

West, Gerald. 1991. *Biblical Hermeneutics of Liberation: Modes of Bible Reading in the South African Context*. Pietermaritzburg: Cluster Publications.

White, Hylton. 1995. *In the Tradition of the Forefathers: Bushman Traditionality at Kagga Kamma*. Cape Town: Centre for African Studies and University of Cape Town Press.

Wilkinson, Jane. 1992 [1990]. *Talking with African Writers*. London: James Currey and Portsmouth: Heinemann.

Williams, Raymond. 1961. *The Long Revolution*. New York: Columbia University Press.

Wylie, Dan. 1999. *Savage Delight*. Pietermaritzburg: University of Natal Press.

———. 2006. *Myth of Iron: Shaka in History*. Pietermaritzburg: University of KwaZulu-Natal Press.

Worthy, Stephen. 1994. 'Never Again: Prophets of da City.' *Hip Hop Connection*: 42–50.

Young, Robert. 2001. *Postcolonialism: An Historical Introduction*. Oxford: Blackwell.

Zinn, Christopher. 1998. 'Bridge too Far for Black Australia.' *Mail and Guardian* 17–23 April.

Index